Federico Iarlori

PARIS CURIOUS

Illustrations by Monica Lovati

RIZZOLI
UNIVERSE

Contents

GETTING STARTED

GETTING AROUND PARIS

A PARISIAN'S WORLD

I LOVE SHOPPING

PARIS ON FOOT

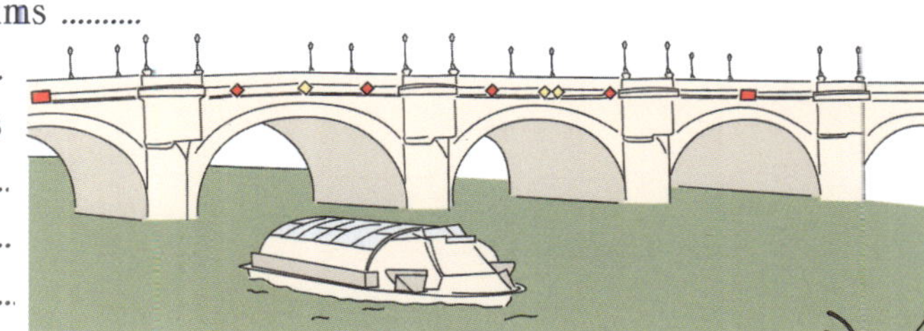

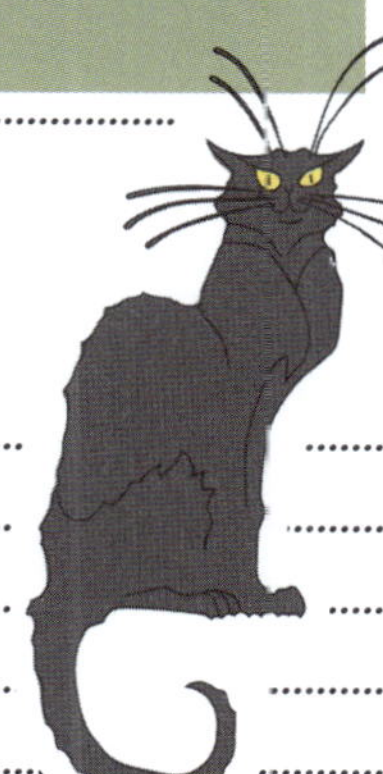

THE THOUSAND FACES OF PARIS

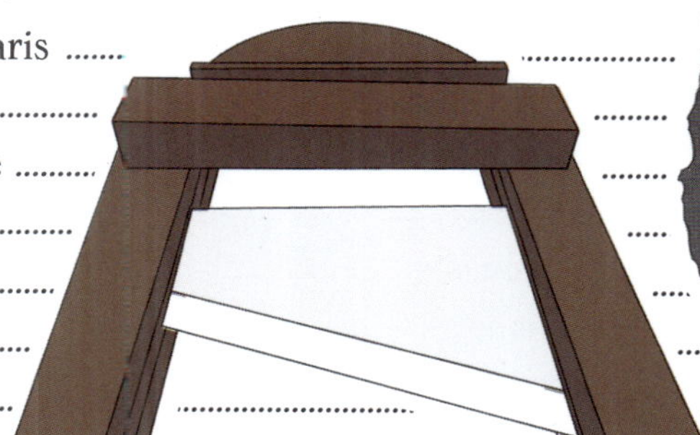

OFF THE BEATEN TRACK

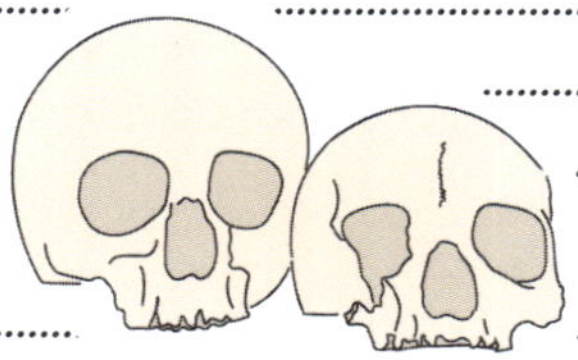

PARIS FROM ABOVE

PARIS AND POP CULTURE

PARIS IN PINK

PARIS AND BOOKS

GETTING OUT OF PARIS

EATING AND DRINKING IN PARIS

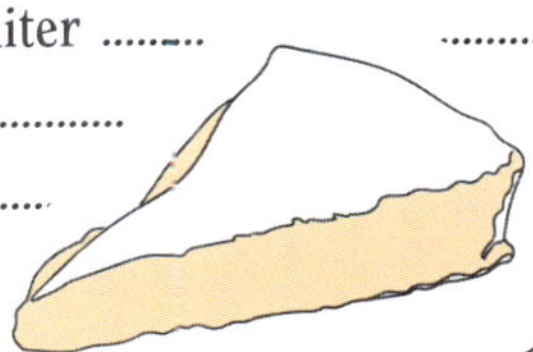

DON'T MISS

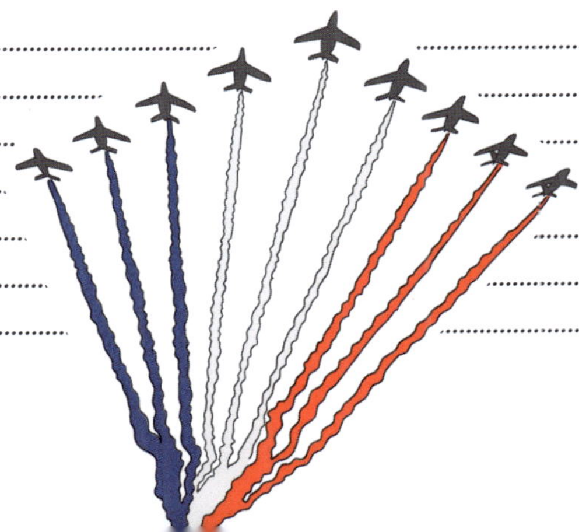

For rue Saint-Denis, which showed me true love.

"Paris, c'est une idée." Léo Ferré

After nearly sixteen years of living in France, I understand what it means to have the ex-pat label stuck on my back. Whenever I meet a French person for the first time, we invariably go through the same routine: they immediately spot my Italian accent and ask me where I'm from. I reply that I'm from Rome (even though I was actually born in a small town in Abruzzo that most Parisians would never have heard of). At that point, they will usually exclaim: "Ah! Rome, the most beautiful city in the world!" Then, with a sly smile, add: "After Paris, of course."

What might simply seem a rather unfunny joke at first is, in fact, a valuable key to understanding certain enigmatic things, such as French people's natural lack of modesty, for example, or their particular sense of humor.

Taking certain opinions for granted (by placing them in the "obvious" category) is an ideal way of both avoiding the need to justify them and converting them into absolute truths. "Paris is the most beautiful city in the world." Period. This established, obvious, incontrovertible, and indeed almost commonplace fact is handed down by osmosis from generation to generation.

The jolt between expectation and reality can sometimes be problematic (such as some Japanese tourists with "Paris Syndrome" who become faint at the very sight of it, or with those who think of Paris as the city of love, only to find their partner has cheated on them there), but it is a good opportunity to set aside one's own naivety and discover that love can be both marvelous and cruel, both here in Paris or anywhere else in the world. In other cases, such as my own (I dreamed of the place as a child, loved it as a student, put up with it as a worker, and hated it as a parent), the matter may be a little more complicated.

The nineteenth-century journalist Alphonse Karr wrote that "a true Parisian doesn't love Paris, but can't live anywhere else," and he was not wrong. Those who live in the city are well aware that it is gray, exorbitantly expensive, chaotic, polluted, alienating, and snobbish, but they also know that they are highly unlikely ever to leave.

By the same token, those who, like me, have lived in Paris and then moved away

to the provinces know that, to quote Ernest Hemingway, "Wherever you go for the rest of your life, it stays with you." Paris is much more than a city; it is an idea, a notion of freedom and style, of creativity and rebellion, and wherever it finds fertile ground, it threatens to take root in your soul forever. It should come as no surprise that the great twentieth-century French poet Louis Aragon once wrote: "Tear out my heart and you'll see Paris there."

Few other cities in the world have the capacity to seduce, realize, and enhance the potential of some of the greatest minds of men and women in the history of humanity, firing the imaginations of poets, writers, painters, directors, and musicians from around the globe and forming the backdrop of the greatest revolutions of our era.

Stroll along its triumphal *boulevards*, thread your way through its elegant *passages* (covered arcades), lose yourself in the streets and alleys of its most, and least, famous districts, and contemplate the symbols of the *grandeur* of a nation that still claims to be at the heart of things, despite the challenges and vagaries of globalization. You will not only be breathing in the air of history and following in the footsteps of its protagonists, you will also be tapping into an archetypal and inexhaustible source of inspiration to sublimate and transform your own human and artistic soul.

Paris is a universe unto itself, governed by mysterious laws and confined to a relatively restricted area when compared with other European and world metropolises.

A thousand different souls live alongside each other in Paris. It is simultaneously the city of ancient kings and of the spirit of '68, of romance and of nightlife and transgressiveness, the city of bohemian and hyper-modern, futuristic districts, of *haute couture* and flea markets, of aristocrats and ordinary folk. It is both conservative and yet progressive and revolutionary.

Living cheek by jowl in such a way creates the very chaos that makes Paris unique. In this electrifying city there is a constant and peculiarly alienating tension that comes from the sense that anything could happen at any moment. Every visitor can become part of this adventure just by taking a seat at a bistro table or on a bench along the banks of the Seine, by sidling into a jazz cellar or getting lost in the corridors of a museum. You may even find yourself in a director's viewfinder or on the canvas of an artist.

And this is precisely why it is key to understand what to expect and where to focus your attention, to name and tick off things that will inspire emotions or curiosity. From the lips of a true Parisian. Or the next-best thing.

All roads lead to Paris

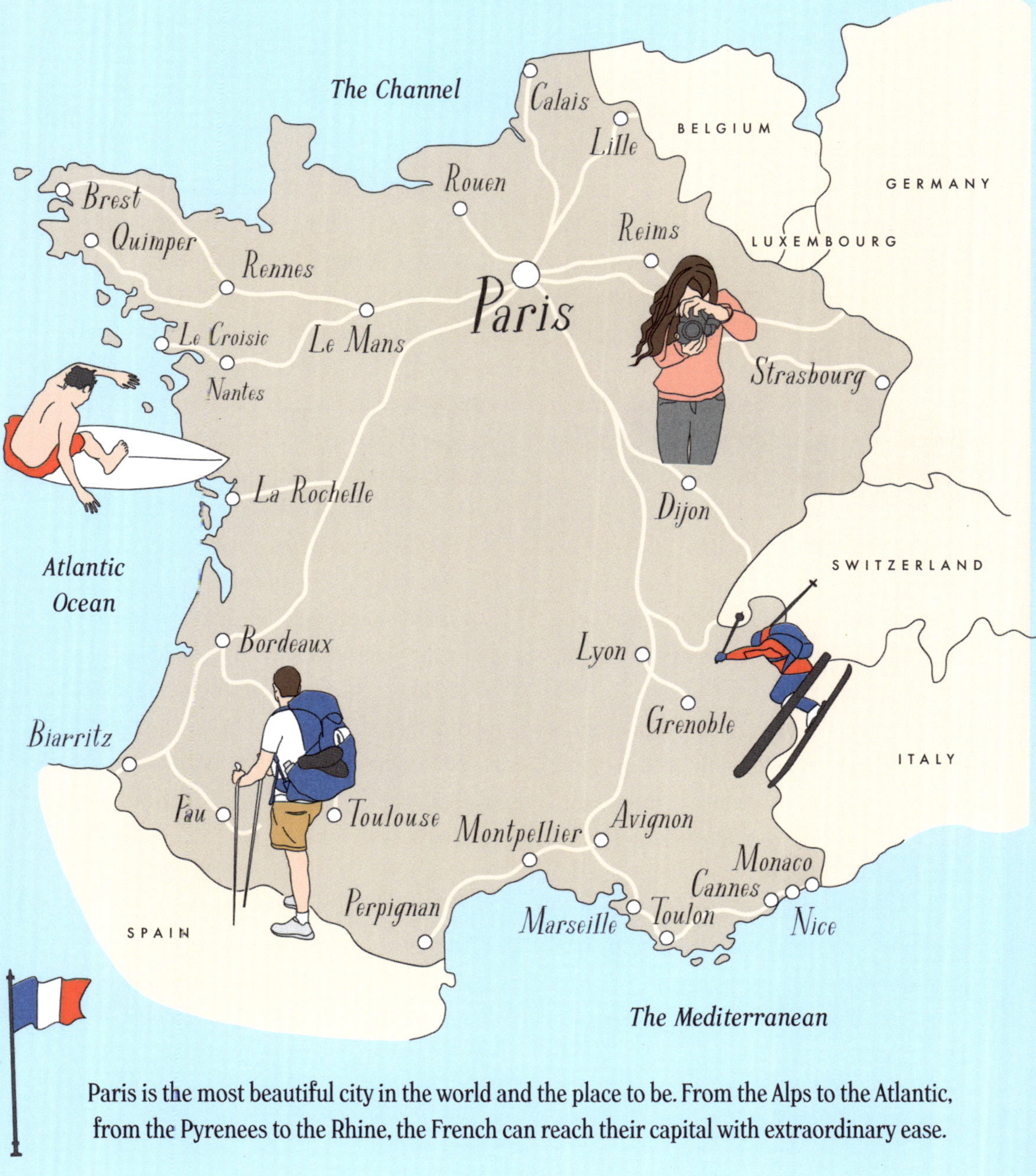

Paris is the most beautiful city in the world and the place to be. From the Alps to the Atlantic, from the Pyrenees to the Rhine, the French can reach their capital with extraordinary ease.

If France were a magnificent galaxy made up of stars and planets, Paris would be at its very center. A single glance at the map of the national rail network, the home of the infamous supersonic TGV, reveals the French capital as a sun, a source of light whose rays radiate out to the farthest corners of the country.

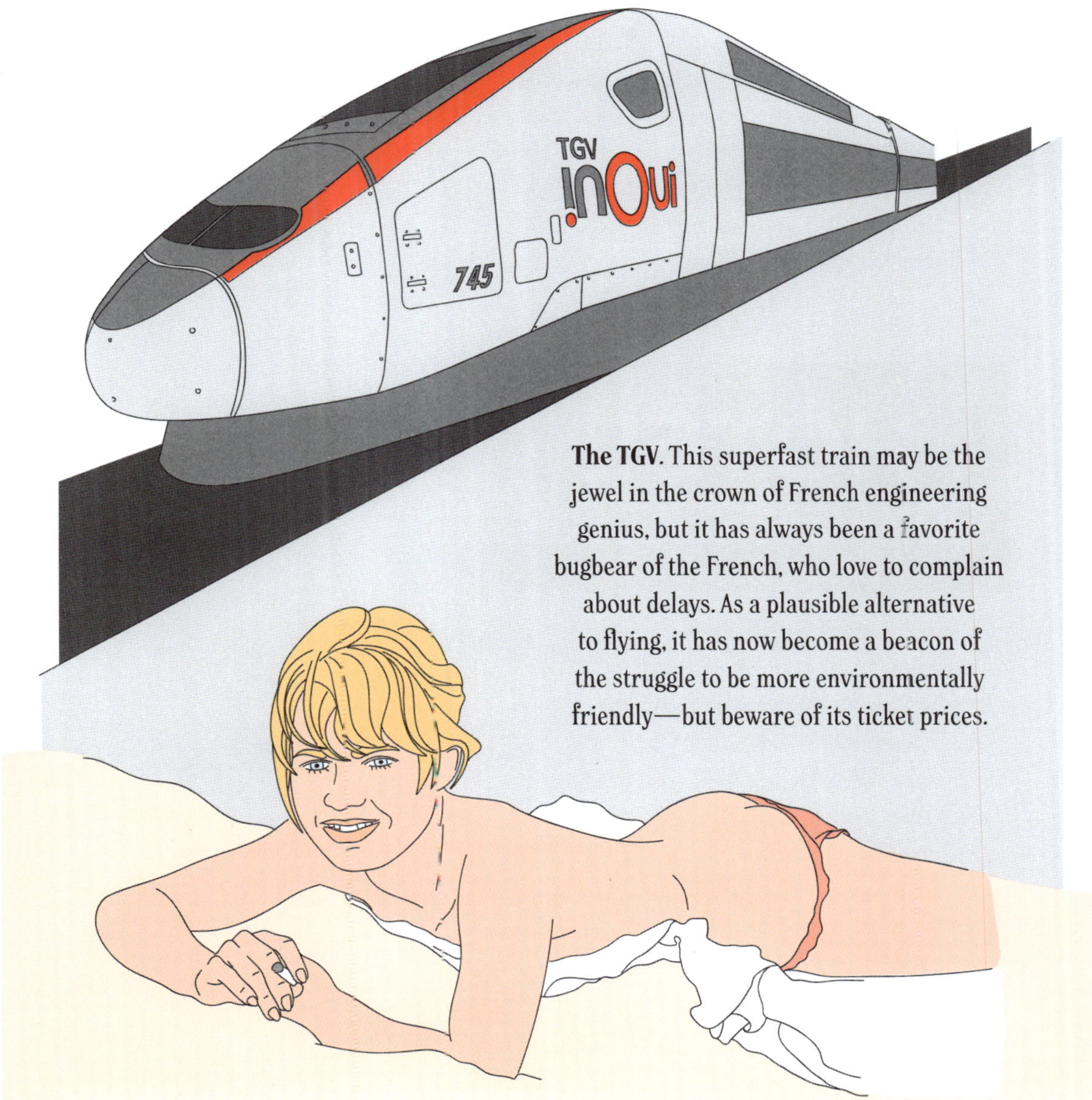

The TGV. This superfast train may be the jewel in the crown of French engineering genius, but it has always been a favorite bugbear of the French, who love to complain about delays. As a plausible alternative to flying, it has now become a beacon of the struggle to be more environmentally friendly—but beware of its ticket prices.

If only Paris were by the sea ... Paris to Marseille is around 500 miles (800 km) and takes under four hours, something for Parisians craving vitamin D to daydream about.

Where to stay

Paris is, of course, one of the most expensive cities in the world, but unlike larger and more sprawling metropolises, it is very compact and homogeneous, so there is no need to stay near the Eiffel Tower to experience the capital's distinctive and unmistakable atmosphere.

Fun fact: It is not widely known that the famous Basilica of Sacré-Cœur in Montmartre is one of the best-value hotels in Paris. A bed costs a few euros (in a dormitory) or a little more for a private room, provided you stay up for an hour at night to pray before the altar.

The efficiency and ubiquity of the city's metro network means that you never feel far from your destination.

Some of the districts that seem more remote (and therefore more affordable), such as the colorful and multi-ethnic neighborhoods of Belleville and Ménilmontant or the areas around Canal de l'Ourcq and the **metro** stops at Château Rouge and Marx Dormoy, may offer a glimpse of a life that is both alternative and at the same time typically Parisian.

Top tip: Look for somewhere to stay near **metro** line M11, especially around Goncourt, Belleville, Pyrénées, or Jourdain stations, as this is one of the fastest lines in the city and will take you from the outskirts to Notre-Dame Cathedral in a matter of minutes.

What to pack

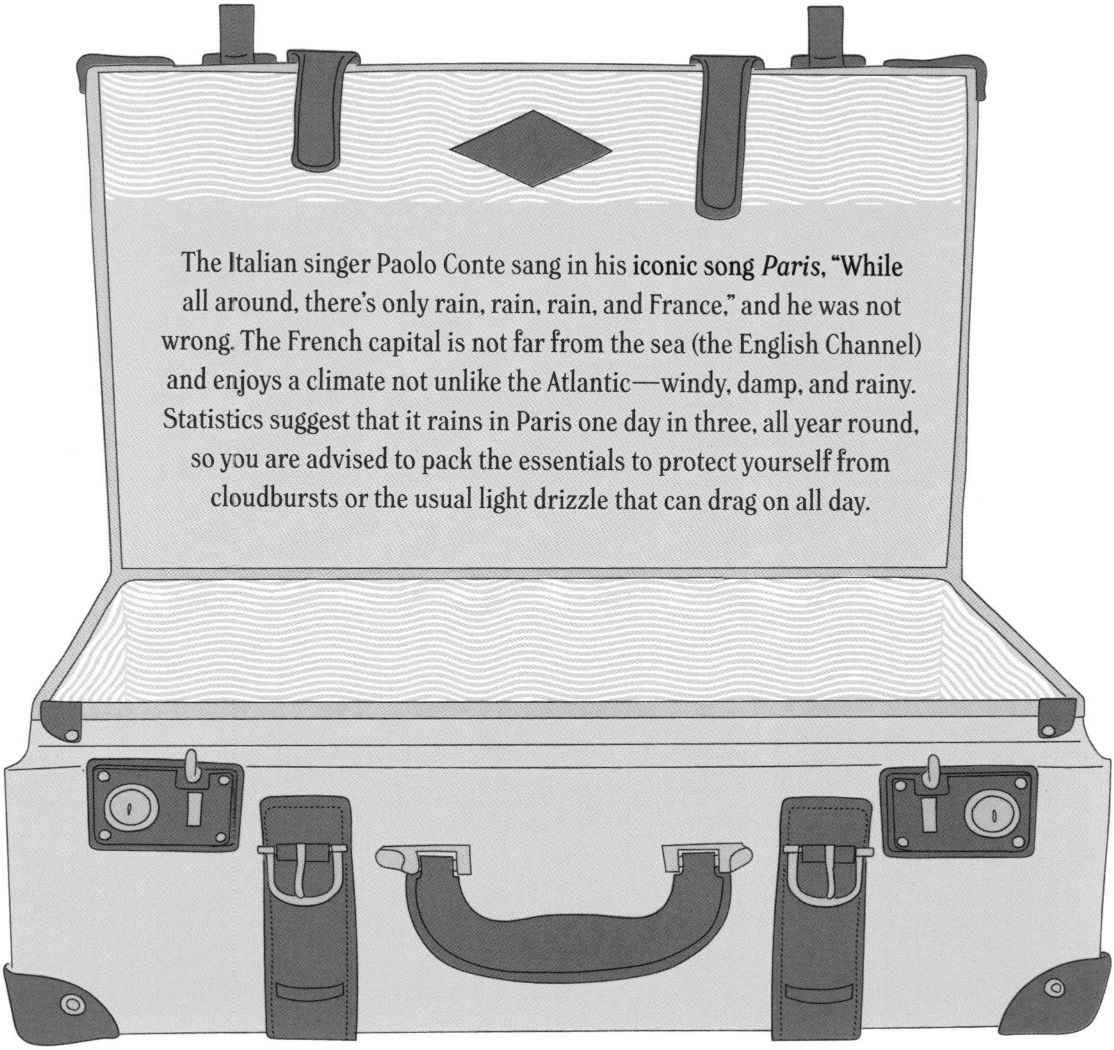

The Italian singer Paolo Conte sang in his **iconic song *Paris*, "While** all around, there's only rain, rain, rain, and France," and he was not wrong. The French capital is not far from the sea (the English Channel) and enjoys a climate not unlike the Atlantic—windy, damp, and rainy. Statistics suggest that it rains in Paris one day in three, all year round, so you are advised to pack the essentials to protect yourself from cloudbursts or the usual light drizzle that can drag on all day.

Top tip: Try not to carry an umbrella if at all possible as many of the sidewalks are quite narrow and crowded. Take some comfortable shoes as there will be a lot of walking, including along endless metro passages that probably hold some kind of world record for architectural obstacles.

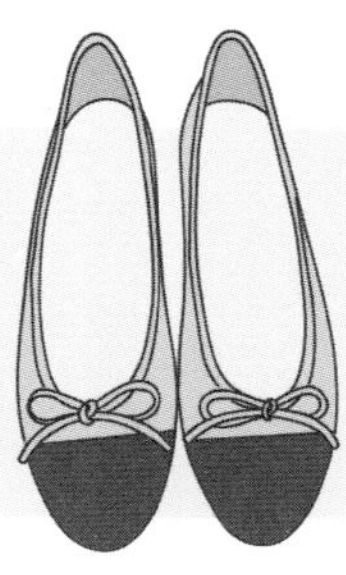

Some good news! Nightfall is much later in Paris than many other European capitals (it's still light at 10 P.M. in summer), so you'll have more time to be a tourist or just to enjoy an aperitif before it gets dark.

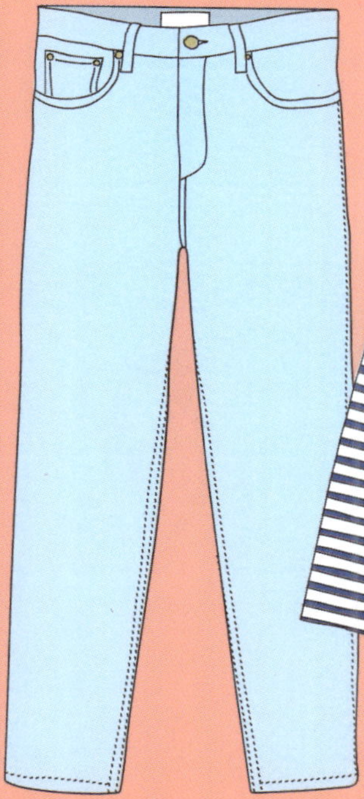

The top five wardrobe items for Parisians: 1) A trench coat (preferably beige), for both men and women; 2) A long-sleeved T-shirt with blue or red stripes (sailor-style); 3) A black leather jacket; 4) Skinny jeans in a light color; 5) Ballet pumps or, more generally, comfortable and lightweight flats, even in winter.

Three golden rules: Dress down, with a "just got out of bed" look, and for women, very subtle makeup and hair, with at most a dash of lipstick and red nails—fingers and toes.

Getting there

You will land at one of Paris's two main airports: the immense maze of Charles de Gaulle (Europe's second-largest airport after London Heathrow) or Orly. Both are about an hour from the city center.

So how do you get from the airport to the city center?

Overground options include shuttle buses or a **taxicab** (if you can spot a genuine one among the horde of unlicensed cab drivers who will mob you at the Arrivals exit), or you can book an Uber (or even an Uber Moto if traveling alone).

Underground travel options include local trains (RER), although do note that these are often packed and/or subject to delays. Luckily enough, Orly airport has been connected to the city center by metro line M14 since 2024 and Charles de Gaulle will be connected by 2030.

Top tip: Steer clear of the Périphérique, which is every Parisian's nightmare. It is an often chaotic and congested ring road.

Connectivity

Paris may conjure up images of romantic black-and-white movies, but it has become a hyper-connected metropolis like any other major city (without losing its vintage soul). Your **smartphone** will notice the difference.

If you're looking for an internet connection, make use of Paris's broadband Wi-Fi network, which is available to all at no charge. You will find this more or less everywhere—in parks, gardens, libraries, museums, and any other public space. If you cannot see a sign, look for the network on the Wi-Fi Finder app. Otherwise, just go to the nearest cybercafe.

If, like me, you are always running low on battery, I recommend heading straight to the nearest bus stop where you will find a USB port that might just save your life.

@ milk

milkprint.fr

If you find yourself without your phone for whatever reason and are in a panic, there is always Milk Les Halles, Paris's largest cybercafe (6,460 square feet/600 square meters), which is open 24/7 for web-surfing, and you can print whatever you like.

Smart apps

Is your **smartphone** charged up and connected? Here are some smart apps to find your way through Paris's urban jungle and make your life easier.

Bonjour RATP. Everything you need to know about Parisian public transport (**metro**, bus, RER, and regional trains), including how to plan the most convenient routes.

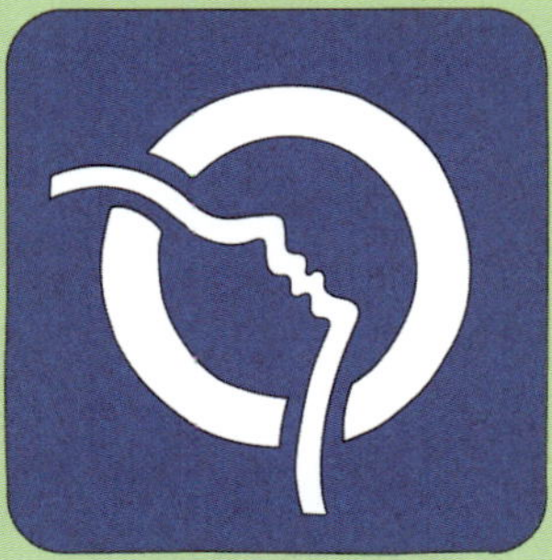

RainToday. You are now aware that it often rains in Paris, so it's best to be prepared. This app will tell you exactly when and where it will be wet, so you can choose whether to go to the park or visit a museum.

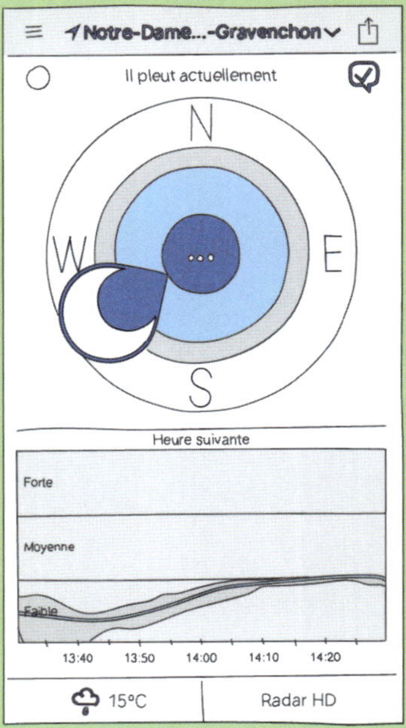

Vélib'. If (like many Parisians) you enjoy getting around by bike, this app will help you find the nearest rental outlet and see in real time how many bicycles (or parking spots) are available.

MisterGoodBeer. Paris is a city of bars and any occasion can be a good excuse for a *demi* (a small beer) or even a pint. This app will find the nearest, cheapest beer and will most likely take you to the least touristy bar you can find.

ICI toilettes. When nature calls, this app will direct you to the nearest restrooms, which may be in places where you can use the facilities for free (although you might have to buy a drink) or a public restroom. You will also be able to find places with baby-changing facilities.

Parlez-vous français?

The French are fiercely proud of their language and are not always fluent in English. If you don't speak French, brace yourself for a cool reception, and if you do, but not well, be prepared to be corrected.

According to a survey published by the *Figaro* daily newspaper, 40 percent of French people consider Parisians to be conceited and arrogant, with only 1 percent finding them friendly.

So now you know who you're dealing with.

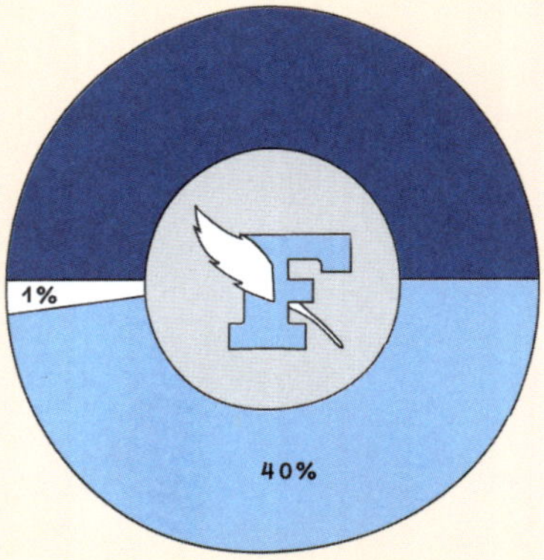

Paris is a multicultural city and Parisians like nothing better than spotting a foreign accent. Sometimes just uttering a single word is enough to prompt the ritual question: "So where is your *charmant accent* (charming accent) from?"

This is, of course, a euphemism.

Even if you do speak French, the meaning of some expressions could well be confusing. This is perfectly normal since they're almost certain to be idiomatic, or *verlan*, a kind of slang originating in the *banlieues* (suburbs) that involves reversing the order of syllables in a word to create a new one.

Examples of *verlan*:

choper (take, catch) = ***pécho***

énervé (angry) = ***vénère***

femme (woman, wife) = ***meuf***

féte (party) = ***teuf***

fou (crazy) = ***ouf***

"Oh, you're Italian? *Hola, bueno*!"

As an Italian, I often find myself in a situation like this, so don't be surprised. To a lot of French people, Italian and Spanish sound very similar.

Using the Métro

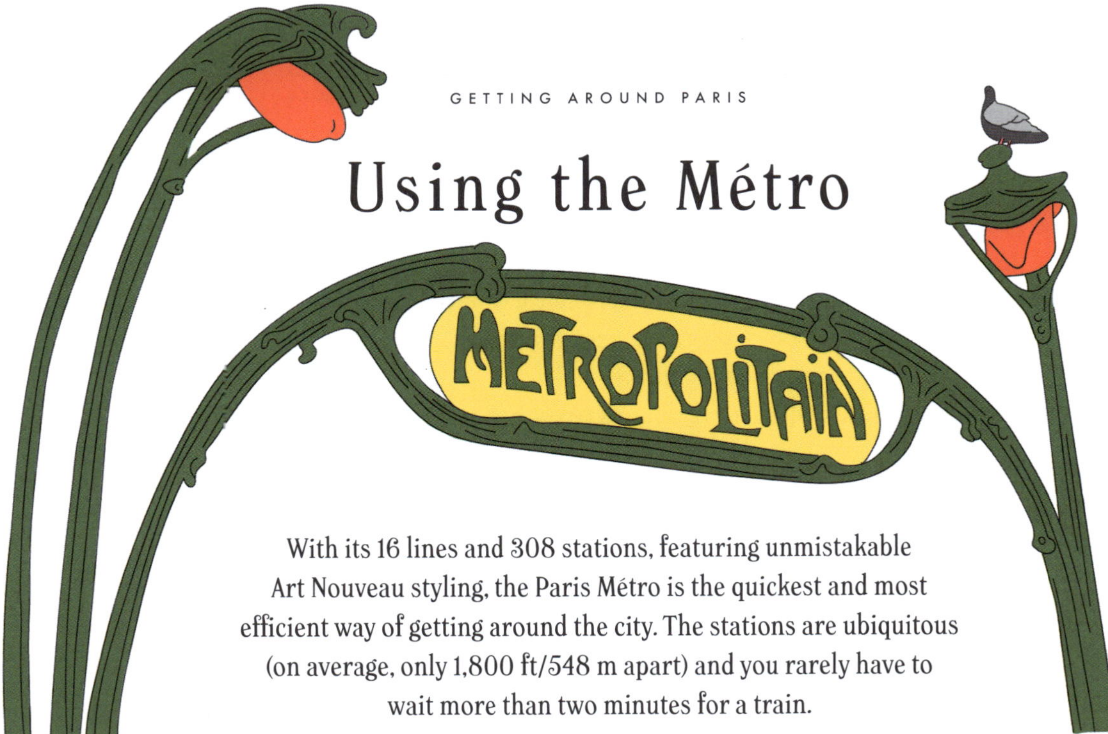

With its 16 lines and 308 stations, featuring unmistakable Art Nouveau styling, the Paris Métro is the quickest and most efficient way of getting around the city. The stations are ubiquitous (on average, only 1,800 ft/548 m apart) and you rarely have to wait more than two minutes for a train.

Fun fact
Parisians spend **92 minutes on public transport** every day, on average.

Have you ever fallen in love at first sight on a **subway** but been unable to summon the courage to make a move? Paris Bulle (now defunct) **and Crushfindr** (still active) were the first prototypical dating sites, inspired by the microcosmic world of furtive glances and silences that exists in the underground tunnels of the city.

Métro-boulot-dodo. This famous expression, meaning "metro-work-sleep," was intended as an ironic description of the daily routine of Parisians.

A foolproof trick. If you want to know how long it will take you to get from one point to another on a metro line, allow 90 seconds for each stop.

Three must-sees when the Paris Métro is traveling above ground:

1) The Eiffel Tower (line M6 between Passy and Bir-Hakeim)
2) Notre-Dame (line M5 between Gare d'Austerlitz and Quai de la Rapée)
3) Bibliothèque nationale (line M6 between Bercy and Quai de la Gare)

Parisian districts (*arrondissements*)

Paris is snail-shaped and subdivided into twenty *arrondissements* that spiral out from the center to the suburbs. For Parisians, of course, each number not only refers to an administrative district but also denotes a universe to which specific clichés are attributed.

"*Elle fait très XVIème*" (she looks very 16th) is a way of saying that someone dresses as if they are rich.

Why are the wealthy Parisians clustered in the west (16th), while the less affluent are in the northeast (18th, 19th, 20th)? During the Industrial Revolution, it seems, the richest people settled in areas shielded from chimney smoke (because of the way the wind blows, which is mainly from west to east). Tough luck for the rest.

Can I get your number?

2nd *arrondissement*: the smallest
5th *arrondissement*: the oldest
6th *arrondissement*: the most expensive
7th *arrondissement*: the richest
10th *arrondissement*: the least touristy
11th *arrondissement*: the most party-going
13th *arrondissement*: Chinatown

The term "21st *arrondissement*" is used to refer to any area outside the Périphérique to which Parisians habitually travel. These include the La Défense district and even the seaside resort of Deauville, on the English Channel.

Back in the days when Paris had only twelve *arrondissements* (before 1859), the expression "I got married in the town hall of the 13th *arrondissement*" meant you were single!

The River Seine

The Seine is the geographical center and economic engine of the city, and also the main axis that divides Paris in two, with the Right Bank to the north and the Left Bank to the south. Since their closure to traffic, the banks of the Seine (a UNESCO World Heritage Site since 1991) have become a favorite place for Parisians to take a stroll.

Paris has its own Statue of Liberty (albeit in miniature) located on the Île aux Cygnes, a splendid man-made island in the Seine with views of the Eiffel Tower that are unjustly overlooked by tourist guides.

In the mood for seafood? Well, just around the corner from the Place de la Bastille is a marina (le Bassin de l'Arsenal) where the city feels far away. Try an aperitif at the Grand Bleu or binge on seafood at Sea Bar Paris Pêche to round off the idyll.

Parisians love Latin American dance, and Jardin Tino Rossi overlooking the Seine (not far from the university quarter) is a haven for salsa addicts.

Fun fact: According to Parisian tradition, if the statue of the Zouave standing at the base of one of the buttresses of the Pont de l'Alma has wet feet, it means that the Seine is in flood.

Don't miss: The Petit Bain, a bar with a view, not to mention a restaurant, concert hall, disco, and more. It is a floating island of culture on the Seine.

Notre-Dame: The heart of Paris

The Cathedral of Notre-Dame is the queen of the Île de la Cité, the island on which Paris was founded, and the most popular monument in France. After the devastation of the fire that shocked every Parisian to the core in 2019, it was restored and reopened in 2024.

On the small square in front of Notre-Dame is Point Zero, the exact spot from which distances to other French cities are measured. For the French, this is, of course, the *omphalos*—the navel or axis, of the world!

Take refuge from the crowds in the gardens of Square Jean XXIII right behind the cathedral, a tranquil spot beside the Seine with a splendid view of Notre-Dame's flying buttresses. In spring, immerse yourself in the wonderful colors of Japanese cherry trees.

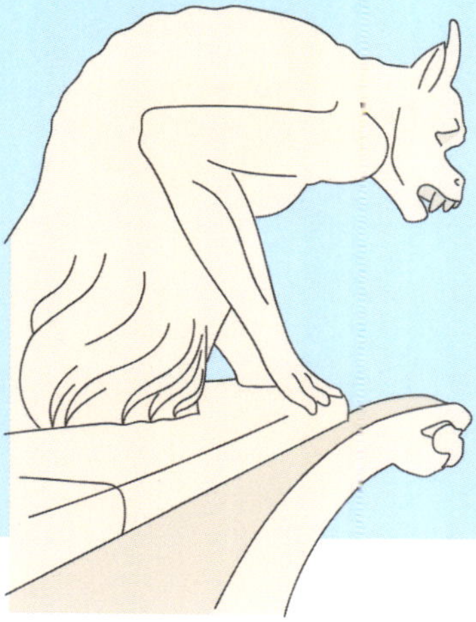

Unlike the famous gargoyles, which allow rainwater to run off, the uncanny grotesques created by the nineteenth-century architect Viollet-le-Duc enjoy the purely symbolic role of deterring demons and dark forces.

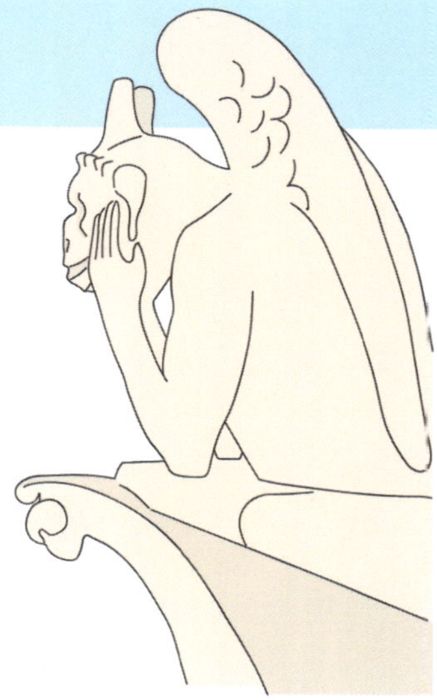

Fun fact: The rooster (the national symbol of France) that once stood on the cathedral's tallest spire contained two precious relics. It miraculously survived the blaze.

It is not widely known that Notre-Dame produces its own honey. Hives were installed on the cathedral roofs in 2013 and now house a total population of 200,000 bees capable of producing 55 lb (25 kg) of honey every year.

Vélib': A different way of getting around

Following suit from their mayor, every good Parisian is also a good environmentalist and a big fan of alternative modes of transport. The legendary Vélib' (pioneers of bike rentals) passed a record total of 400,000 subscribers in 2020.

If you live in "the highlands" (i.e., in areas like Ménilmontant or Montmartre), watch out, since Vélibs are rather heavy vehicles. It's a better idea to go for an electric "Véligo" for climbing hills.

A record number of bikes (18,215!) was logged along the Boulevard de Sébastopol on September 6, 2022. Despite the growing numbers of bike lanes, gridlock is the order of the day, even on two wheels.

If you prefer to set off on foot, remember that a true Parisian rarely waits for the green signal to cross the street. By the same token, no motorist or indeed cyclist will stop to let you cross, so be bold!

Top tip: If you get the chance, rent a Vélib' at night and roam through the semi-deserted streets of the city center before crossing the Cour Napoléon courtyard in front of the Louvre. You won't regret it!

The infamous French *politesse*

Bonjour

For the French, and Parisians in particular, formality is very important. In order to avoid appearing uncultured, always begin every exchange with a *bonjour* and end with a *s'il vous plaît* when entering and leaving a store.

S'il vous plaît

While in some countries it is now customary to use casual forms of address, even with strangers, this is still considered a sign of disrespect in France and it is much better to use the formal *vous* with everyone.

Bonne journée

The *formules de politesse* are expressions used by the French to express politeness in the written and spoken language. When you leave a venue in the morning, don't forget to wish everyone a *bonne journée*; in the afternoon a *bonne soirée*; and on Fridays a *bon week-end*.

And don't forget!

If you usually hold the door open for women as they enter or leave, be prepared for a startled look of disbelief. In France, politeness can be taken for sexism.

Pas mal

AMAZING!

Sympa

Parisians dislike excess (synonymous with vulgarity) and prefer moderation. Unlike for Americans, nothing reaches heights of being "Awesome!" At best, it's *pas mal* (not bad) or *sympa* (quite nice).

Parisian manners are formal and restrained.

Meet the Parisians: The grumbler

The French, and Parisians in particular, often complain about everything: the food in restaurants. other people, **the Paris Métro, their** jobs, politicians, neighbors, you name it.

The *râleur* (grumbler) is a Parisian *par excellence*, even with little cause for complaint.

A survey based on emoticons sent on Messenger has shown that Paris is the grumpiest city in France. The top spots in the listings are all held by cities in the north of Europe, showing the key role that clouds and cold must play.

A Parisian syllogism. 1) A person who complains is someone who has identified a problem. 2) A person who identifies a problem is intelligent. 3) Therefore, a person who complains is intelligent. Corollary: Anyone who is always happy with their lot might just be a little daft.

The Parisian paradox. 80 percent of Parisians are proud of Paris and no fewer than 93 percent love their city, but two out of three say they want to leave—one day.

According to a national survey, the top three reasons for the French to complain are: 1) Bureaucratic problems; 2) Transport delays and strikes; 3) Action by the government of the day.

The equally infamous French *grandeur*

Many believe that France is the most beautiful country in the world, French is the most beautiful language in the world, Paris is the most beautiful city in the world, and French wines are the finest in the world, as are the cheeses. Once these points have been settled, we can start talking about who might come next in the rankings.

By *grandeur*, literally "greatness," we mean the real or percieved idea that France holds a superior position among nations. This belief can reflect genuine national pride but sadly can also be used as an argument in cultural and political propaganda.

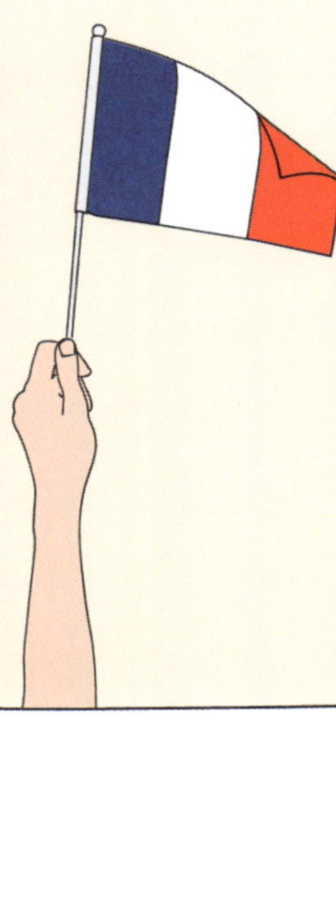

Some French people have a noticeable sense of superiority as far as other francophone countries are concerned, in particular toward Belgium and Quebec. Quite unfairly and without grounds, these countries might be looked down on for their intelligence or accent, even though these perceptions are not well founded.

By the same token, the French have some nice expressions for when someone gets a little too big for their boots: *avoir la grosse tête* (having a big head) and *prendre le melon* (taking the melon), or even *avoir les chevilles qui enflent* (having swollen ankles).

"France couldn't be France without *grandeur*." Charles de Gaulle

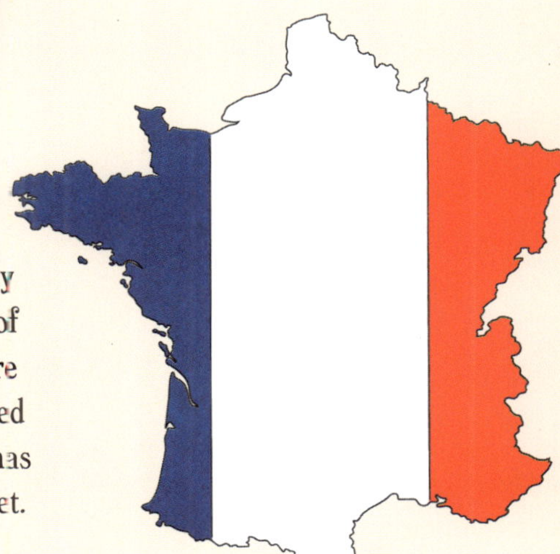

Fun fact: France is the largest country in the European Union, with an area of 213,000 square miles (551,000 square km). In addition, because of its so-called DROM-COMs (see below), the country has a presence in every ocean on the planet.

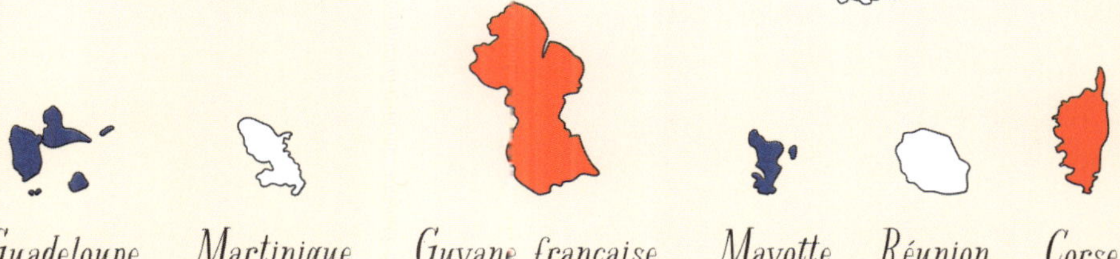

Meet the Parisians: The revolutionary

From the French Revolution to the *gilets jaunes* (yellow vests—protesters in 2018–2020), Parisians have never needed much of an excuse to take to the streets against those in power or, indeed, conversely, to stay at home. Strikes, in particular are a common occurrence.

With an average of 114 days lost to strike action every year, France can claim to be world champions in this particular discipline, followed by Belgium and Canada.

True Parisians tend not to go for an overly polished or *bourgeois* look. There are more important things in life, like the class struggle or global warming. Men might sport a designer three-day stubble, while women will opt for an effortless but curated "bed-head" look.

The expression *refaire le monde* (putting the world to rights) refers to the delight the French typically take in long conversations. Translated literally, it means "remaking the world," which reveals the expression's subversive intentions against established order.

Parisians are politically correct (in public, at least), so watch out, as expressing a "divergent" opinion that doesn't quite align with progressive ideals might see you called a *facho* (fascist).

Conversation is a sporting event in Paris, a tug-of-war based on relentless disagreement, and a winner and a loser is baked into the outcome, so if you just intend to make jokes or waste time, don't even bother.

The French baguette

PAIN À LA

The baguette is an iconic symbol of France recognized around the world. As far as the French are concerned, their bread is indeed sacred and inimitable, and in Paris in particular it is worth queuing round the block for at the best bakery in the neighborhood. A baguette must be eaten fresh from the oven.

A baguette has different names according to its shape: if it's thicker, it is called a *flûte*; if thinner, a *ficelle*; and if a bit shorter, a *déjeunette*.

The term *tradition*, however, refers to a baguette made without any additives and is used to distinguish homemade bread from industrially produced fare.

Who invented the baguette?

There are three theories: 1) Napoleon's bakers may have created it to make bread easier for soldiers to carry. 2) It was invented in Vienna and imported to France in the nineteenth century. 3) While the Paris Métro was being built, a kind of bread was devised that did not need to be cut with a knife in order to prevent workers from being injured in the frequent fights that were breaking out.

FARINE DE MEULE

If you order a baguette in a bakery, the baker might even ask you how you want it: *bien cuite* or *pas trop cuite*? (well done or not so well done). The Parisians really can be obsessive about their bread.

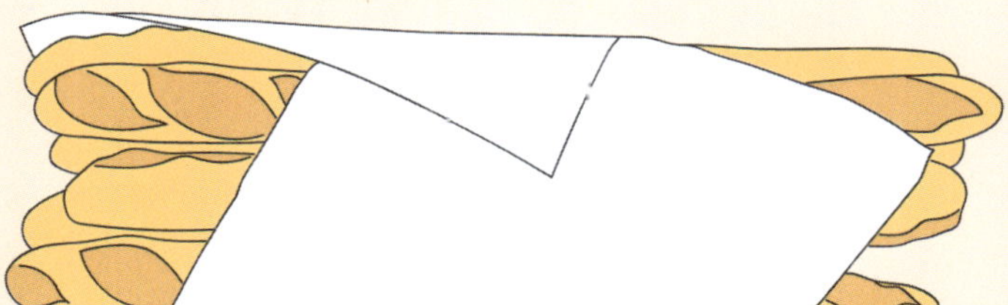

FABRICATION TRADITIONNELLE

Drinking coffee in Paris

Parisians have a different relationship with coffee than, say, Europeans or Americans, for example. It is not just a quick shot gulped down while standing at a bar. You need to take your time, and it's often an excuse to sit down at a small table outside a bar, on your own or in company, and read, write, or chat without having to keep one eye on the clock.

Un café (or *un express*) in France is halfway between an *espresso* and an Americano. The cup shape would be familiar to any Italian but is filled to the brim. If this idea fills you with horror, ask for a *café bien serré* and you'll get something like a *ristretto* (a half-filled cup).

Coffee shops in Paris also offer other types of coffee such as *un allongé* (an espresso with double the water) and *café crème* (a shot of espresso with steamed milk and a frothy top), as well as the usual Americanos and cappuccinos.

Café filtre. The undefeated coffee champion in every French home until the advent of capsule machines. This technique involves filling a filter (usually made of paper) with ground coffee and pouring boiling water over it.

Café gourmand. If you're in two minds about indulging in a dessert or unsure what to choose, this could be the ideal compromise. Go for a coffee with a small selection of *petit-fours.*

The French obsession with an *apéro*

An aperitif is a non-negotiable, not just in Paris but throughout France. Aperitifs are enjoyed straight after work (before you even go home) and there is a real threat of continuing late into the night, skipping supper entirely.

The concept of a drink with snacks is not the norm, however. The most you can often hope for at a table in most bars is a tiny bowl of peanuts.

If you pick the right place, however, you can order a *planche mixte*, a sharing platter of charcuterie and cheeses.

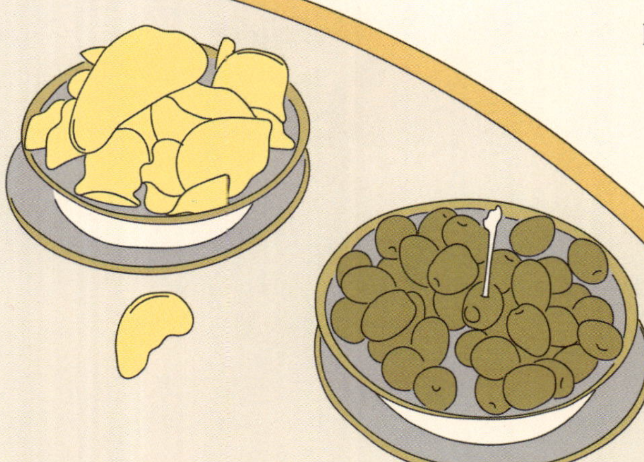

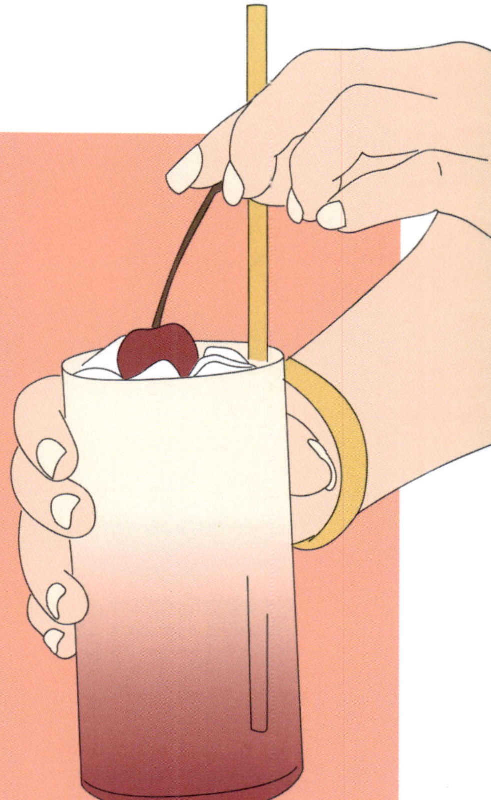

What are we drinking? The usual go-to is a glass of wine, of course, or a draft beer (usually *un demi* or a small glass). Another classic (more common in the South of France) is a *pastis* diluted with water, while mojitos and spritzes are also becoming more popular.

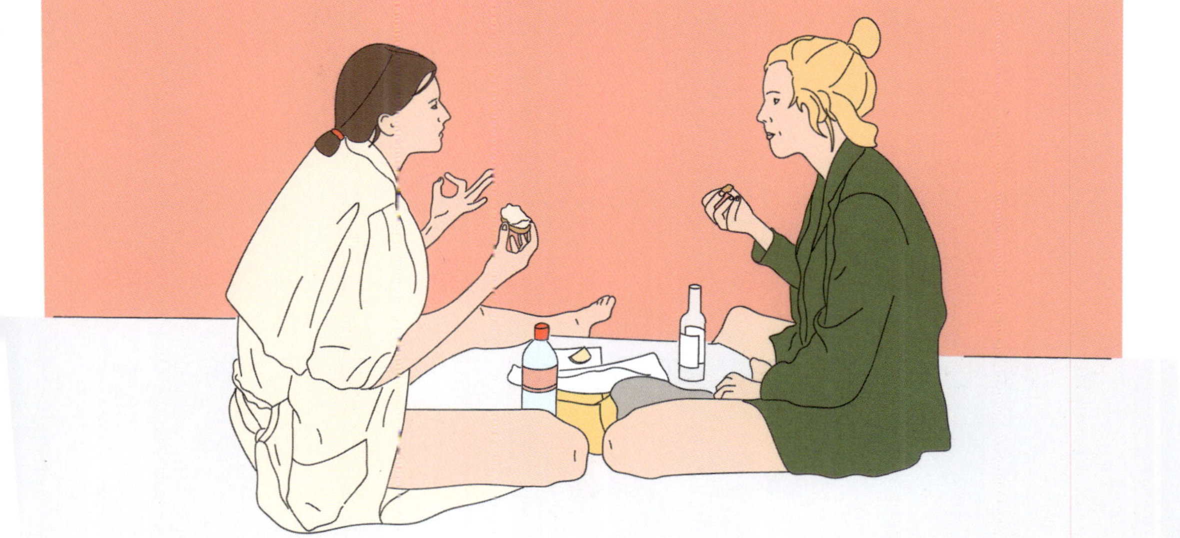

Weather permitting, Parisians love to combine an aperitif with a picnic on the banks of the Seine or along the canals that have been built through the city (the Saint-Martin or Ourcq, for example) and are also very fond of a game of *pétanque* or *kubb.*

Brunch: Another Parisian obsession

For Parisians, Sunday is not Sunday without a *grasse mat* (lie-in) and brunch, an Anglo-Saxon habit that took over the capital a few years ago, supplanting the classic French breakfast of coffee, a *tartine*, and a *croissant*.

La France qui brunche. An expression that refers to the so-called *bobos* (bourgeois-bohemians, generally affluent and left-leaning voters) who are often criticized by right-wing commentators. Brunch is also a status symbol.

Although Parisians can sometimes be a bit snobbish toward Americans, it's also no secret that they love New York, which is younger, more dynamic, and a bit more "underground" than their beloved old Paris.

Having brunch with friends is a little more New York-y and a little less *franchouillard* (dyed-in-the-wool French).

The Sunday blues. Parisians don't like Sundays because everything is closed, Monday is just around the corner, and they risk having nothing to say to their colleagues. The only two ways of saving the day from *déprime* (depression) are a trip to the movie theater or a spot of brunch with friends.

Meet the Parisians: The *bobo* and the *bomeur*

The ***bobo*** (a contraction of *bourgeois* and *bohemian*) is a classic Parisian character. They tend to be creative types, working in journalism, communications, fashion, or the arts, and they are inclusive and eco-friendly, eating organic produce, reading the *Libération* newspaper, and voting with the left (but not with the far left).

Branché. This term translates literally as "connected" and refers to a place or person (and this may even include the *bobos*) that is trendy and fashionable, as opposed to anything that's *ringard* (i.e., old and corny).

The ***bomeur***, a contraction of *bourgeois* and *chômeur* (unemployed), is a variation on the *bobo* theme. These too are creatives, but they "work" alone, often at a small table in a bar, and will invariably have a brilliant project on the go that may well come to nothing.

Where do they hang out? Bobo central is to be found in the 11th *arrondissement*, while the *bomeurs* have now been banished to Montreuil and Pantin, out beyond the Périphérique.

Parisian vocabulary

Parisians are a breed apart from the rest of France, and have their own typical behavioral and linguistic tics.

Putain

This slang term can carry either positive or negative connotations depending on context. However, it is considered vulgar and best avoided in tourist settings as it can be offensive.

Sympa

If the Parisians like a situation, a bar, or a show, they will call it *sympa* (quite nice), but nothing more.

It is important not to let yourself get carried away with enthusiasm.

Parisians are understated and minimalist, and everything is *petit* (small/little) as far as they are concerned: *un p'tit café, une p'tite bière.*

Petit

Anything *gros*, however, is vulgar and decidedly un-Parisian.

Abbreviations: *Déj'* for *déjeuner*, *insup'* for *insupportable* (unacceptable), *déso'* for *désolé* (sorry), and so on. Parisians will shorten a word at the drop of a hat.

Anglicisms (franglais): *Trop cool, c'est boring, je green-lighte, je speede, je suis dead, je suis over-booké, c'est has-been* ... suddenly, you're in New York!

Five Parisian idioms (and their literal translations):

1) *Être charrette* (to be/do a cart): To be running late or overwhelmed with work.
2) *Entrer à l'œil* (to get in on the eye): To get in free.
3) *Ça passe crème* (it goes like cream): It works like a charm.
4) *C'est canon* (it's cannon): It's magnificent.
5) *Se mettre la tête* (to put on one's head): To get very drunk at a party.

Les Halles: The belly of Paris

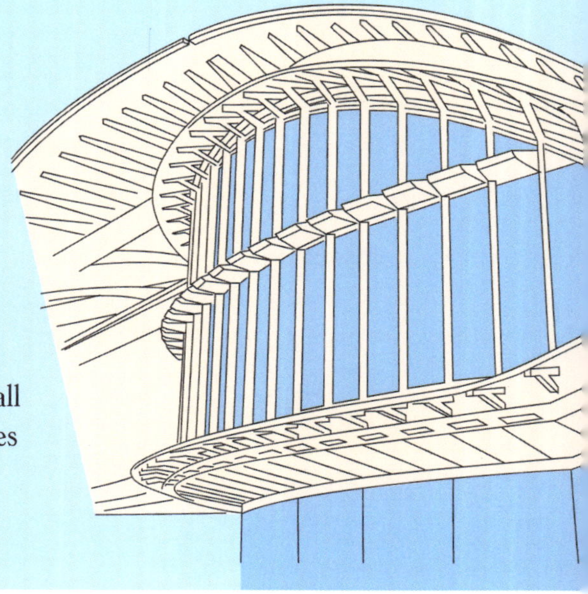

Once the main wholesale market for food produce and described by Émile Zola as the "belly of Paris," the ultra-modern shopping mall of Les Halles is one of Parisians' favorite places for shopping and culture.

Nestled in the heart of Paris, Les Halles is the third largest shopping mall in France and boasts the busiest swimming pool in the capital. With no fewer than twenty-seven screens (and a specialist media library), it's also a mecca for cinephiles.

A stroll around the neighborhood (1). The Galerie Véro-Dodat is a little-known covered arcade that is rarely busy, although it is one of the most picturesque, its Neoclassical lines and old-school boutiques guaranteeing you a real trip back in time.

A stroll around the neighborhood (2). The pedestrianized zone of rue Montorgueil is one of the oldest and most charming in Paris. Don't miss the historic Stohrer pâtisserie or, if oysters are more your thing, the Au Rocher de Cancale restaurant.

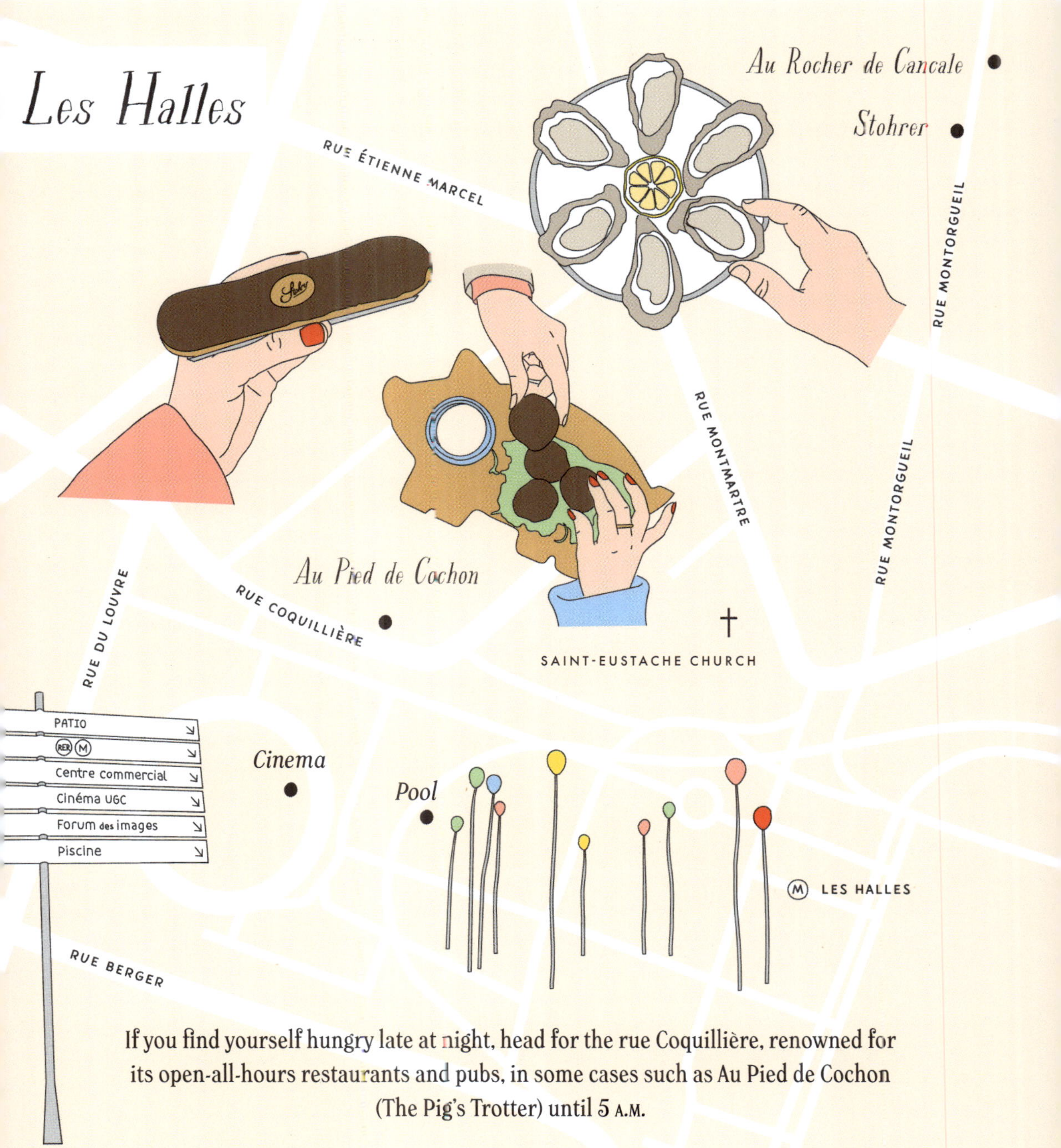

If you find yourself hungry late at night, head for the rue Coquillière, renowned for its open-all-hours restaurants and pubs, in some cases such as Au Pied de Cochon (The Pig's Trotter) until 5 A.M.

Department stores

Shopping malls as we know them today were invented in Paris in the first half of the nineteenth century. As symbols of the Industrial Revolution and the advent of what became known as consumer society, they are now no longer mere temples of shopping but genuine works of art, and among the finest examples of Art Nouveau architecture.

The oldest. The "cathedral of modern commerce," as Émile Zola described it in his 1883 novel *Au Bonheur des Dames* (*The Ladies' Paradise*), Le Bon Marché was the first department store in history and, in my opinion, still has the best food hall in the capital.

The best view. Head up to the bar/restaurant on the seventh floor of the Printemps department store and treat yourself to one of the most beautiful panoramic views of Paris.

SAMARITAINE

The most picturesque. The splendid building housing the Samaritaine department store looks out over the Seine and the legendary Pont Neuf. It underwent sixteen years of restoration work a few years ago and is officially listed as a national historic monument.

Galeries Lafayette

Even if you have no intention of doing any shopping, you should still drop into the Galeries Lafayette to check out the splendid Art Nouveau dome atop the main atrium. It is totally worth it.

The Champs-Élysées

This majestic thoroughfare, probably the most famous in Paris, runs for $1\frac{1}{4}$ miles (2 km) between the Place de la Concorde and the Arc de Triomphe. A mecca for shoppers (especially those seeking luxury goods), it is less popular with some Parisians and is now considered rather kitsch.

Top tip (1): Even if you know you'll never be able to afford anything, check out the Louis Vuitton "cathedral shop," essentially a museum with free admission.

A stroll along the Champs-Élysées should include one small but essential detour, a trip to the Grand Palais and the Petit Palais. The capital's most beautiful exhibitions are often hosted within these Art Nouveau masterpieces. A spectacle within a spectacle.

Fun fact: The Champs-Élysées is closed to traffic on the first Sunday of every month. Impromptu picnics are held by the roadside and children play ball games, adding to the already rather surreal atmosphere.

Top tip (2): Be sure to try the famous macarons from Ladurée, and for maximum enjoyment, order them in the café. Even if you are already familiar with macarons, it will be like eating this very French sweet treat for the first time all over again.

Shopping on a budget: Thrift stores

Paris is home to many thrift stores that sell secondhand clothes at affordable prices. They have now become a symbol of environmentalism and the fight back against fast fashion.

Être stylé. Being stylish in Paris means getting creative and sourcing original outfits that stand out from the crowd. Lots of students, for example, see vintage stores as the perfect place to find something trendy without breaking the bank.

Paris's large thrift stores *(friperies)*, with their creative and diverse clientele, are not just retail outlets but also "social laboratories" that are regularly scrutinized by top couturiers seeking inspiration as they anticipate fashion trends.

La Friperie Solidaire. By collecting used clothes and fabrics, even if damaged, and employing a workforce that is "returning to the workplace" to repair and recycle items for resale to the public, the social enterprise work of retailers like Emmaus is a classic example of a virtuous circle.

Vintage Paris: Flea markets and garage sales

Parisians love vintage, not just clothes but anything from furniture to the most ridiculous (and, sometimes useless!) items, and browsing through antique shops and secondhand stores is a favorite pastime, especially at weekends.

Flea markets. The name derives from the parasites that infest old, shabby clothes. You are likely to find almost anything at almost any price. The most famous are in Saint-Ouen and Porte de Vanves.

Garage sales. *Vide-grenier* literally translates as "attic-emptying," and these are markets in city centers with stalls where private citizens can sell their items. Download the *Vide-greniers et brocantes* app to find out when and where to find them.

Cabinets de curiosités. Inquisitive visitors may not be able to resist visiting one of these unusual outlets inspired by the *Wunderkammer* (rooms of wonder) of past collectors. You are likely to find anything and everything, from stuffed animals to archeological finds.

Sunday shopping: Le Marais

Le Marais is the capital's oldest and most famous Jewish quarter, so most stores and venues are open on Sundays, too. It is full of thrift stores and bijou boutiques selling fashion and designer goods, and the perfect place to find surprising and original pieces.

If you're not sure where to start, head for the rue Vieille du Temple and the rue des Francs-Bourgeois and dive straight in.

Top tip: If you fancy a snack, pop to Sacha Finkelsztajn, the famous yellow bakery (Polish-Jewish delicacies), or try the legendary falafel at L'As du Fallafel in rue des Rosiers. You might have to queue, but hang on in there!

And it's not all about shopping. Two of Paris's most beautiful museums are located in Le Marais, the Musée Carnavalet (Carnavalet Museum), which chronicles the history of Paris, and the Musée Picasso (Picasso Museum), both housed in splendid town houses.

Don't miss: The Marché des Enfants Rouges (Market of the Red Children), with its stands selling delicacies from all over the world, is one of the oldest and most picturesque covered markets in Paris and the ideal spot for a lunch that's a little bit out of the ordinary.

Parisian boulevards

Paris's majestic and seemingly endless boulevards are among the most iconic of the city's symbols and were the instruments with which the powers-that-be redesigned the city's geometry, freeing it from its medieval roots and catapulting it into modernity.

Tell me what floor you live on, and I'll tell you who you are. 1st floor: stores and businesses; 2nd floor: retail storage or concierge's apartments; 3rd floor: rich families; 4th and 5th floors: the lower-middle classes; 6th floor: poor families; mansard attics: servants and students.

The *Inception* effect. It would not be a boulevard **without Georges-Eugène Haussmann's** typical town houses, which always adhere to their creator's golden rules: their height is proportional to the width of the street (with a maximum of six floors) and is consistent along the entire length of the street.

Comédie de Boulevard

Comédie de boulevard. Boulevard theater was named in honor of the frivolous and carefree spirit of the first theaters to be founded along Paris's boulevards. The plays are lighthearted and fast-paced.

Fun fact: Many streets are called *rue* before the boulevard and *rue du Faubourg* (outside the borough) after crossing it, and this once marked the boundary between the city and the countryside. It is a handy way of finding your bearings.

Parisian arcades

Twentieth-century German philosopher Walter Benjamin used the term "arcades" as a symbol of the modern world in his eponymous project (*Passagen-Werk* or *Arcades Project*), but Paris's *passages couverts* (arcades) are enchanting, covered pedestrian streets carved through the heart of Parisian town houses, teeming with stores, bars, and restaurants.

The oldest: Passage des Panoramas. One of the first covered arcades to be built in Europe, now renowned for its stamp dealers and postcard stores.

The most elegant: Galerie Vivienne. Feast your eyes on the mosaic flooring, the refined glazed roof, and the sublime porticos, just round the corner from the Palais Royal. Glorious.

The most Parisian: Passage Jouffroy. This was the first of its kind to be built entirely of iron and glass. Lovers of antique books and top-quality stationery will be in heaven.

LE PASSAGE DE PONDICHÉRY

The most exotic: Passage Brady. Known by locals as "Little India," this is the ideal place to find inexpensive, exotic items and eat the finest curry in Paris.

Le Procope

My favorite: Cour du Commerce Saint-André. In proper *rive gauche* (Left Bank) intellectual style, this open-air arcade is where you will find Le Procope, the oldest café in Paris, among other attractions.

HÔTEL CHOPIN

Museums: The Great Classics

You will find some of the world's most beautiful museums in Paris, so make the most of them, especially if you're not just passing through. Many offer free admission on the first Sunday of the month.

The **Louvre** has the paradoxical virtue of being overwhelmingly vast. I'd suggest visiting the Cour Carrée—its largest courtyard, best seen at night—with its sculpture galleries, where Canova's works are unforgettable, and the rooms devoted to French painters.

The **Musée d'Orsay** (Orsay Museum) is housed in a wonderful old train station that is worth the price of admission on its own. Don't forget to take a selfie silhouetted against the glass clock face, and the *pointilliste* paintings on the top floor are a must, not to mention various works by Monet and Van Gogh.

CINÉMA

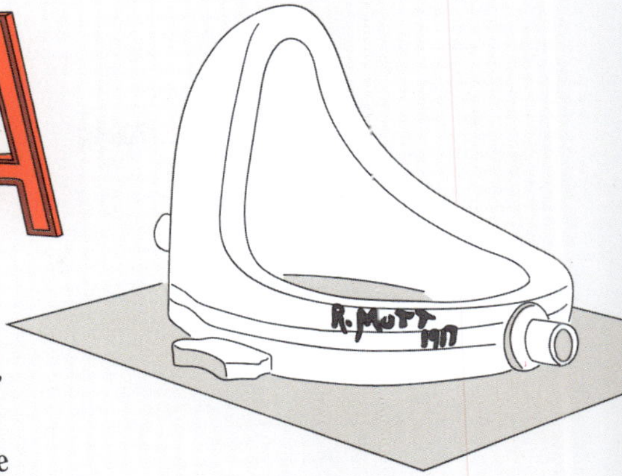

Centre Pompidou. In addition to its invariably topical, creative, and stimulating exhibitions, the Pompidou Center is the most popular museum with locals because of its library, much beloved of students, and its movie theater screens dedicated to arthouse films.

It was Claude Monet himself who selected the **Musée de l'Orangerie** (Orangery Museum) as the place to exhibit his famous *Water Lilies*—eight panels, each 6 ft × 300 ft (2 m × 91 m). These two oval rooms arranged like a *lemniscate* (infinity symbol) in the heart of the Tuileries Garden are unmissable for art lovers.

Other must-see museums

These museums are a bit off the beaten tourist track. but they promise a more human and engaging experience.

Musée Rodin. With interest revived by Carla Bruni's splendid turn as a tour guide in Woody Allen's 2011 movie *Midnight in Paris*, the Rodin Museum and garden dedicated to the French sculptor is an oasis of tranquility and beauty that is worth a visit.

Fondation Louis Vuitton. Boasting a futuristic building designed by architecture superstar Frank Gehry and a location just round the corner from the immense green lung of the Bois de Boulogne, this cultural space is a must-see for any lover of design and contemporary art.

The **Atelier des Lumières**, housed in an old foundry in the 11th *arrondissement*, offers immersive, interactive experiences of masterpieces and digital art to be enjoyed by both adults and children.

The **Musée de Cluny** (Cluny Museum) is in the heart of Paris and recently underwent extensive renovation and modernization. The evocative setting of this celebration of medieval art blends the timeless fascination of ancient Roman bathhouses with contemporary architecture.

Parks and gardens

In a city like Paris, where the population density exceeds that of Seoul, green spaces are not a luxury but a necessity and a matter of survival. Fortunately, there is no shortage of options.

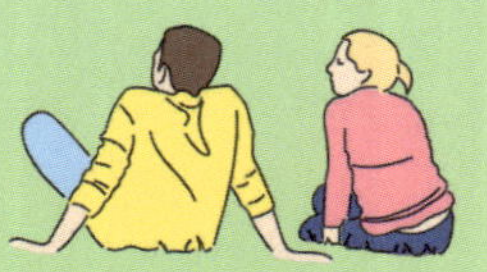

The most popular: Parc des Buttes-Chaumont. Boasting hillside views over the city, a small lake, and a couple of waterfalls, the park is overrun by Parisians at the first glimpse of spring sunshine. Definitely worth a visit, but not if you are looking for a bit of privacy.

The biggest: Parc Floral is 70 acres (28 hectares) of greenery in the heart of the Bois de Vincennes and the ideal place to escape the chaos of the city for some quality time with the family. The mini-golf courses are particularly beautiful.

The most literary: The grounds surrounding the Maison de Balzac (Balzac's House), the museum in the former residence of the nineteenth-century French novelist Honoré de Balzac, are one of Paris's many secret gardens. A tranquil and discreet place with a view of the Eiffel Tower.

The most elegant: Parc Monceau. With its gates, towering trees, arches, and columns located in one of Paris's fanciest *arrondissements*, this is an archetypally French garden.

Cemeteries to the stars

Paris's cemeteries are not just places of remembrance, but also somewhere to enjoy a stroll. Appreciate the architectural beauty as you walk around the last resting places of the great and the good.

Jim Morrison and Oscar Wilde at Père-Lachaise. These are non-negotiable stops in Paris's biggest cemetery. Leave an "alternative" memento for the legendary Doors frontman and leave a lipstick kiss by the grave of the Irish writer.

Baudelaire and Sartre & Beauvoir in Montparnasse. Fans can leave their verses at the graveside of the most iconic Decadent poet of them all, or inspect the tomb of Paris's most famous intellectual couple.

Dalida in Montmartre. This cemetery is more intimate than the two previous ones and houses the grave of the famous Italian-French singer, guarded by a life-size statue looking out toward the sunrise (and the house in which she chose to take her own life).

Pet Cemetery. This cemetery in Asnières, the first for animals to be opened in France, also boasts a roster of stars, from German Shepherd Rin Tin Tin of Hollywood fame to Clément, the dog belonging to French writer Michel Houellebecq.

Bridges of Paris

The bridges of the French capital are both an integral part of an urban landscape dominated by the Seine and authentic works of art in their own right, serving as sources of inspiration for artists of every era and much-loved vantage points from which to view the city.

The oldest: Pont Neuf. Despite its name (New Bridge), this was the first construction to span the Seine in its entirety, inspiring everyone, from painters such as Turner, Renoir, and Monet to movie directors such as Robert Bresson and Leos Carax.

The most casual: Pont des Arts. A typical footbridge over the Seine, not far from the Louvre, and a classic meeting point for young Parisians on their way to a scenic picnic in the center of town. Renovated in 2023 with wooden flooring and padlock-proof glass, so people can no longer attach a "padlock of love."

The most monumental: Pont Alexandre III. With its quartet of gilded bronze statues and a host of friezes, ornamental features, and Art Nouveau lampposts (not to mention a highly Instagrammable view of the Eiffel Tower), this is a must-see for any self-respecting *flaneur* (urban stroller).

The most cinematic: Pont de Bir-Hakeim. The opening scenes of *Last Tango in Paris* were shot here, as was an electrifying sequence in the more recent movie *Inception*. This two-story metal bridge is an incomparable architectural achievement.

Île Saint-Louis

The little Île Saint-Louis is often unfairly neglected in favor of its larger neighbor the Île de la Cité, but it is more residential and far less touristy, providing a focal point of charm, tradition, and elegance in the heart of the capital.

Some essential stops on the Île Saint-Louis:

Berthillon. Many consider this the best ice cream in the world, although it almost certainly needs an Italian perhaps to sign off on this!

Rue Saint-Louis en l'Île. A street of art galleries and a haven for any art lover.

L'Île St. Louis

Pont Marie. One of the oldest and most romantic bridges in all Paris. Despite being rather small, it was once the site of several homes built there in the past, only to be destroyed in a flood that claimed more than fifty lives.

PONT MARIE

A man-made paradise. Among the marvelous *hôtels particuliers* (mansion houses) is the Hôtel de Lauzun, in which Baudelaire and Gautier founded the Club des Hashischins, a group dedicated to experimenting with drugs.

QUAI D'ANJOU

Hôtel Lauzun

RUE SAINT-LOUIS EN L'ÎLE

QUAI DE BÉTHUNE

Square Barye. A triangular space at the tip of the island with access to the Seine and splendid views of the river, which splits into two arms at this point. An ideal place for a relaxing picnic.

Barye Park

PONT DE SULLY

Canal Saint-Martin

This man-made canal, along with the many little bars and bistros scattered along its length, was made popular by the cult 2001 French movie *Amélie* and has become a destination for young Parisians, often turning into an open-air party in spring and summer.

Quai de Valmy. This shopping street runs along the canal and is home to boutiques mostly selling fashion, art, and design. Drop in to the Artazart bookstore, a neighborhood institution.

Cité des Sciences. Take a stroll down the canal away from the city center and you will come to the Bassin de la Villette, the heart of the futuristic Science Village, with its unmistakable Géode, loved by kids.

3 unmissable places: 1) Hôtel du Nord: Not just a bar/restaurant, this is a national treasure that is too beautiful and too iconic to miss.

2) Point Éphémère: A meeting point for local night owls. In summer, head up to the rooftop bar!

3) Le Centquatre-Paris: A cultural and social center that epitomizes Parisian style. The Bal Pop event held here one Saturday a month sees everyone dancing for free. *Allez y*!

Chinatown

The 13th *arrondissement* is largely known for its enormous gray tower blocks. The Quartier asiatique, dubbed "Chinatown" due to its predominantly Asian population and culture, is actually an extremely diverse neighborhood with some unexpected (and well-hidden) attractions.

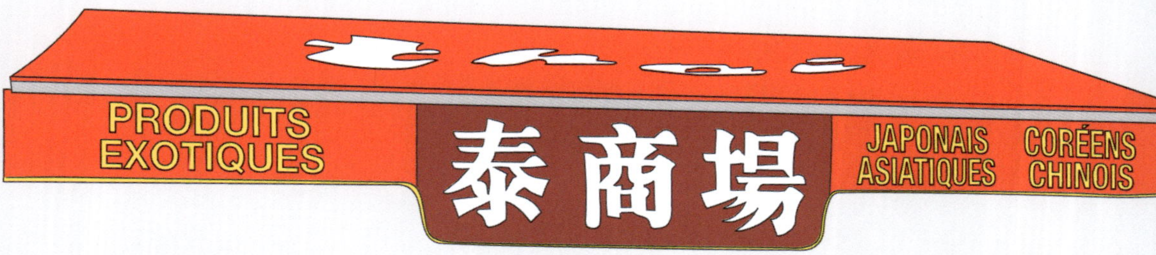

La Butte-aux-Cailles. This low hill overshadowed by skyscrapers used to be a country village, complete with windmills and a vineyard. Everything around it may have changed, but the architecture and the rustic feel of the area have been preserved.

With its post-industrial design, the public swimming pool on the *butte* is one of the most beautiful in Paris, and also boasts one unique feature: thanks to the heat generated by the underground servers used by the Stimergy startup, the water temperature is kept at a steady 82°F (28°C).

Little Alsace ... At no.10, rue Daviel, you are suddenly confronted with an unexpected garden city of half-timbered houses. It's like stepping over the border with Germany.

... and Little Russia. The fourth floor of the apartment block behind no.22, rue Barrault, is a surreal, terraced row of small houses with gabled roofs. These were once inhabited by the drivers of a **taxicab** company, almost all of whom were of Russian origin.

Roman (and medieval) Paris

Lutetia, which was captured by Julius Caesar from the Celtic Parisi tribe, developed into an important Roman city before becoming the largest metropolis in Europe in the medieval period. There are few traces left of this distant past, but they are all the more significant because of this.

Arènes de Lutèce (Lutetia Arena). The remnants of this Gallo-Roman amphitheater in the heart of the 5th *arrondissement* are the earliest evidence of human habitation in Paris. The site is now a popular lunching spot for local workers.

Thermes de Cluny (Cluny thermal baths). The impressive ruins of the Roman thermal baths, just down the road from the Sorbonne, are the most extensive monument from the Gallo-Roman period north of the Loire.

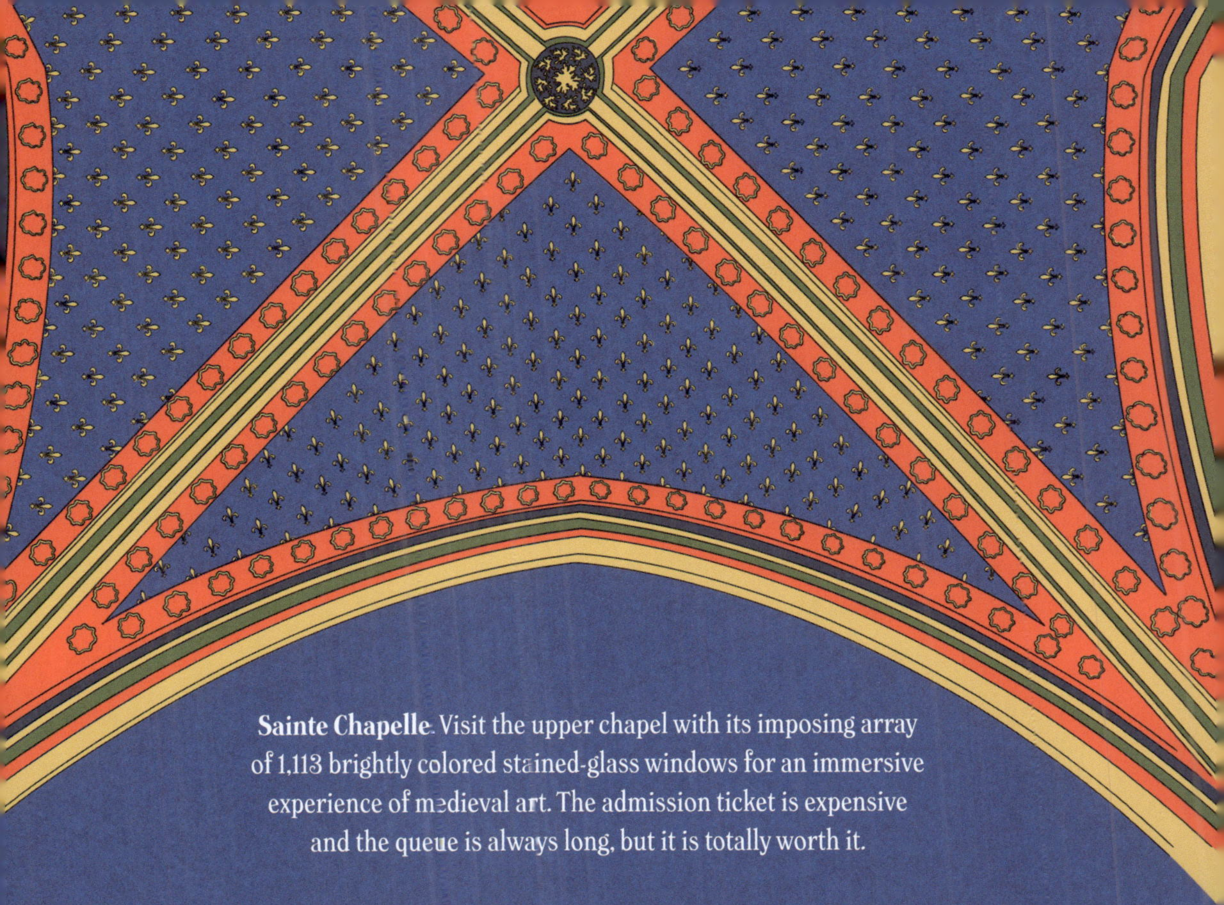

Sainte Chapelle. Visit the upper chapel with its imposing array of 1,113 brightly colored stained-glass windows for an immersive experience of medieval art. The admission ticket is expensive and the queue is always long, but it is totally worth it.

MAISON DE NICOLAS FLAMEL ET DE PERNELLE SA FEMME

Harry Potter would love it. No.51, rue de Montmorency in Le Marais is the oldest house in Paris (1407), once belonging to the famous alchemist Nicolas Flamel, who is said to have discovered the philosopher's stone.

Royal Paris

The French may have beheaded their king, but the monarchs of France were, in fact, the architects of the very *grandeur* that now makes the country so proud. It is perhaps no coincidence that their enthusiasm for the *homme providentiel* (man of destiny) has continued unabated.

Basilique Cathédrale Saint-Denis (Basilica Cathedral of Saint-Denis, aka the necropolis of kings). This (former) abbey church located just beyond the Périphérique is the last resting place of forty-three kings, thirty-two queens, and sixty-three princes and princesses, interred in the largest sculpted funerary vault in Europe.

Once upon a time, there was the guillotine. More than 1,200 people were brought in tumbrils to the splendid Place de la Concorde (which was rechristened Place de la Révolution in 1792), including Louis XVI and Marie Antoinette. A similar fate awaited more than 1,300 unfortunates in the Place de la Nation, which was known at the time as Place du Trône-Renversé (Square of the Upended Throne).

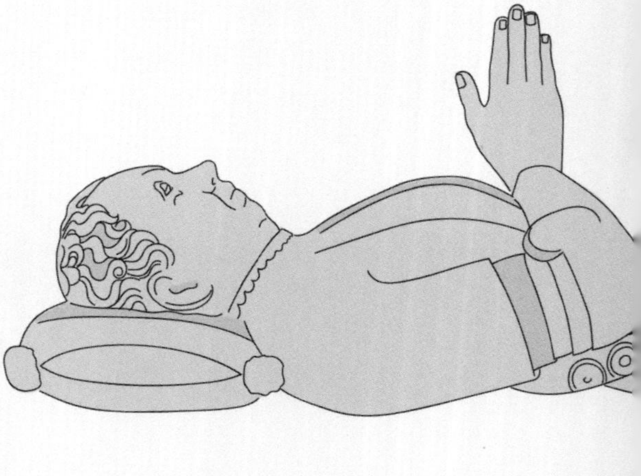

Palais Royal. The scene of the assassination (by a royalist) of le Peletier, the Count of Saint-Fargeau, who had voted for the execution of the king, is now a popular tourist site in Paris, thanks to its famous *Colonnes de Buren* (an artwork by French artist Daniel Buren).

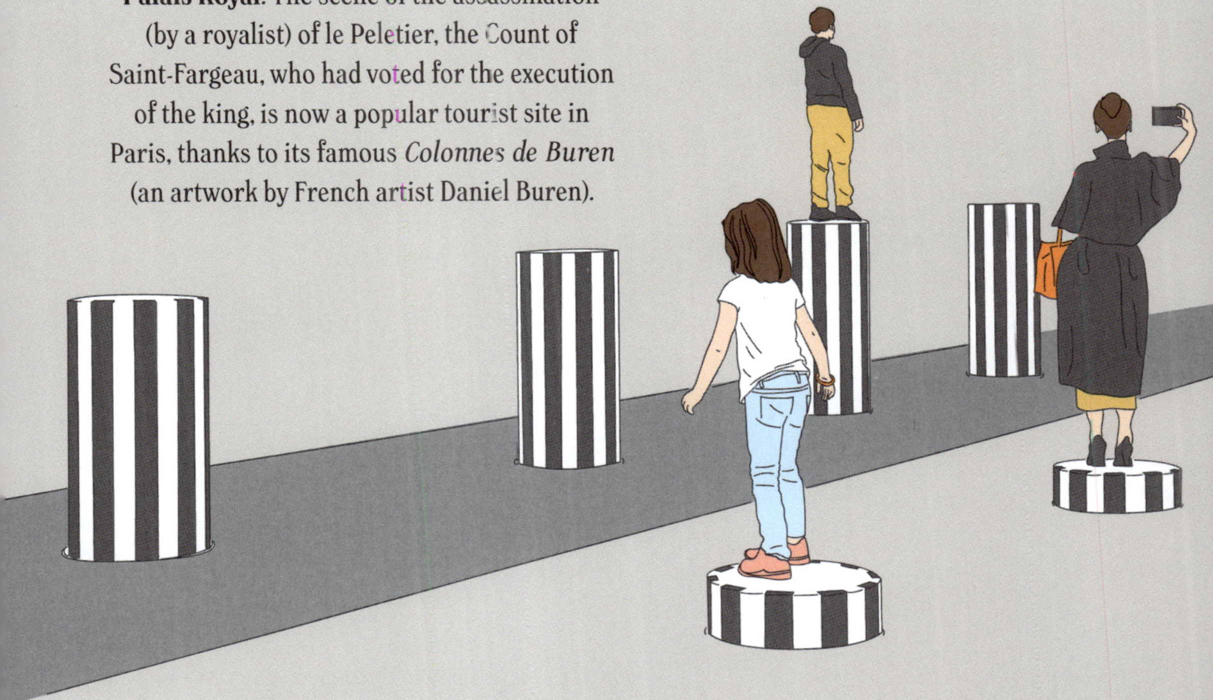

Two symbols that no longer exist. 1) The Palais des Tuileries, Louis XVI's last residence, was destroyed by fire in 1871 and never rebuilt. 2) The Bastille, the emblem of the Revolution, was razed to the ground and "replaced" with the *Colonne de Juillet* (July Column).

Paris in the Belle Époque

Paris became a temple to Art Nouveau style and a symbol of the so-called Belle Époque, the period straddling the late nineteenth and early twentieth centuries that marked a time of peace, economic prosperity, and technological advances.

Pigalle. This became the epicenter of the French idea of fun, thanks to its historic cabarets such as the Chat Noir and the Moulin Rouge, and even today it is a destination for night owls.

The Lavirotte Building. This original and exuberant apartment block at no.29, avenue Rapp has become an icon of Art Nouveau style. Look out for the phallic shape of the main door and the many other sexual allusions worked into the busy facade.

RESTAURANT

Three unmissable places where you can immerse yourself in the Belle Époque:
1) Le Bistrot du Peintre, a delightful and traditional restaurant in Art Nouveau style.
2) Le Train Bleu, a restaurant in the magnificent Gare de Lyon and one of the best-preserved locations from the Paris of the turn of the twentieth century.
3) Le Jardin du Petit Palais, where you can step back in time with its mosaics, colonnades, and *fin-de-siècle* fripperies.

CINÉMATOGRAPHE

Le Cinématographe. The movie industry was born in Paris during the Belle Époque. The very first screening to charge an entrance fee, *La Sortie de l'usine Lumière* (Employees leaving the Lumière factory), was held at the Grand Café on the Boulevard des Capucines in 1895.

Existentialist Paris

Existentialism was a philosophical movement imported into France in the 1940s but also, and most importantly, a lifestyle adopted by the young Parisians of the time, based on hedonism, feminism, and liberation from bourgeois convention.

Saint-Germain-des-Prés. This former student quarter, once overflowing and rebellious, has undergone extensive gentrification and become one of the most expensive areas of the capital, as well as a bastion of Paris's cultural oligarchy.

Café de Flore. This café in Saint-Germain-des-Prés was much loved by Sartre and his colleague (and partner) Simone de Beauvoir. It became the headquarters of the Existentialists and although now largely a tourist attraction, it has not lost its symbolic value.

Jazz cellars. Club Saint-Germain, Tabou, and the Caveau des Lorientais are just some of the local subterranean venues where the Existentialists raved the night away.

Jazz may have moved on, but it's not dead yet, and one place to try is the Caveau des Oubliettes!

From Juliette Gréco to Taylor Swift. The American artist shot the video for *Begin Again* on Place de Furstenberg and in the La Palette café. The most carefully styled pop star of today is picking up the baton from the most "disheveled" in the history of the neighborhood.

Student Paris

Thanks to the international prestige of its universities, Paris has more students than any other city in France.

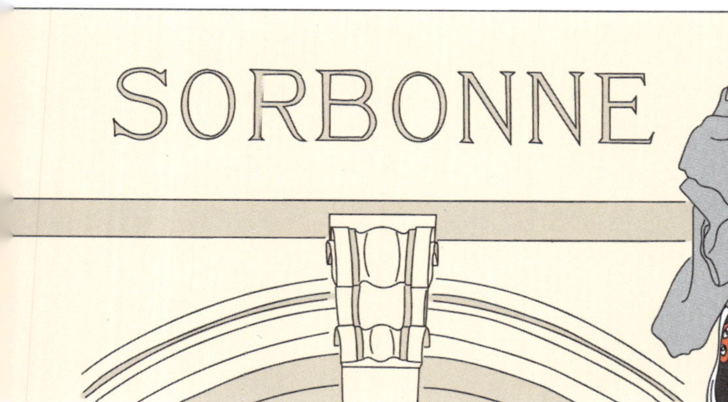

Moving to the capital is almost a foregone conclusion for many young French people (and others), despite the increasingly prohibitive cost of living.

La Sorbonne is the oldest university in the world after Bologna, in Italy. The original seat of the institution (the Maison Mère) in the heart of the Latin Quarter is a magnificent edifice and well worth a visit. See if you can borrow a student ID card to get in.

May '68. The infamous student revolution, with all its demonstrations, barricades, and violent confrontations with the police, began at the Sorbonne and spread like wildfire throughout the Latin Quarter and, ultimately, the entire nation, culminating in the general strike of May 13.

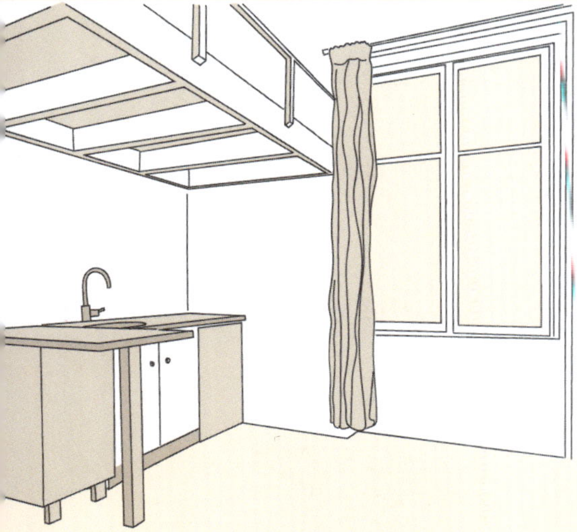

Le studio. The kind of accommodation typically available for students in Paris is a tiny garret apartment in the attic of a Haussmann town house, perhaps under 110 square ft (10 square m) in size, and sometimes without a bathroom. Spoiler alert: The rent still costs a bomb.

Cité U. With 84 acres (34 hectares) of grounds and forty-seven campus houses in surprising designs, from the gigantic pagoda of the Maison du Japon to Le Corbusier's Fondation Suisse, this sprawling university campus welcomes students from across the globe.

"Arty" Paris

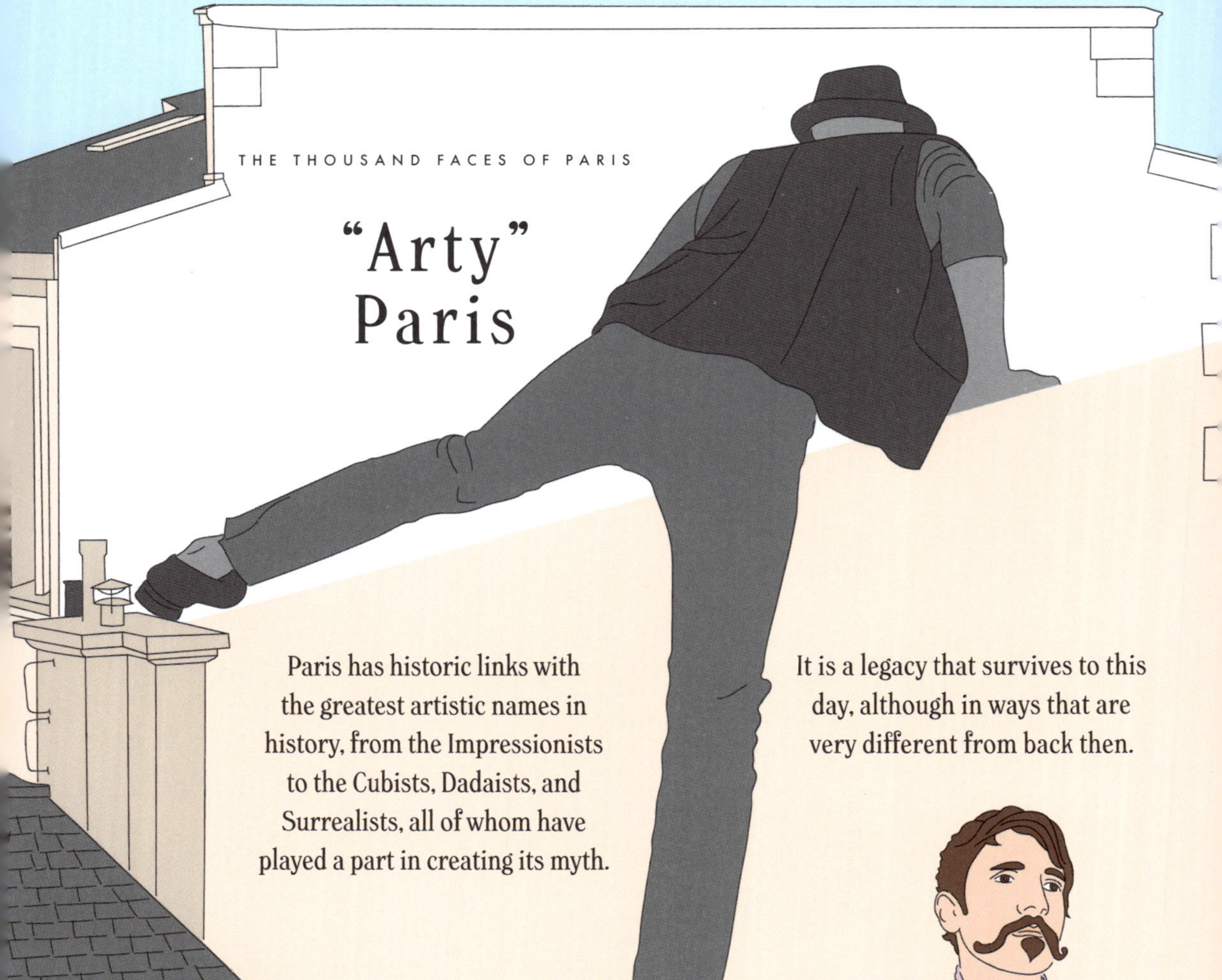

Paris has historic links with the greatest artistic names in history, from the Impressionists to the Cubists, Dadaists, and Surrealists, all of whom have played a part in creating its myth.

It is a legacy that survives to this day, although in ways that are very different from back then.

59 Rivoli. This building in the very middle of one of Paris's main shopping drags is the stuff of legend, a crazy constellation of workshops inhabited by bohemian artists from around the world.

Street art. Paris is covered in the tags of the greatest international street artists from the 13th *arrondissement*, which is practically an open-air museum, through the neighborhoods of Oberkampf, Belleville, and Ménilmontant to the Canal de l'Ourcq. If this is your thing, let the experts at Fresh Street Art Paris be your guide.

La Cinémathèque. A haven for cinephiles and home to the Museum of Cinema, along with arthouse screening rooms, conference facilities, masterclasses, and retrospectives.

LA CINÉMATHÈQUE FRANÇAISE

GROUND CONTROL
libres & curieux

Ground Control. With its food-trucks, pop-up stores, concerts, exhibitions, workshops, and areas dedicated to sports and gardening, this enormous cultural and community center has something for everyone.

Paris by night

New York may be the city that never sleeps, but Paris is no stranger to burning the midnight oil. There is a dizzying array of bars, dance clubs, discos, and gig venues to choose from, but even a stroll through the streets at night delivers some wonderful sights.

Oberkampf. Rue Oberkampf and the surrounding streets (such as rue Jean-Pierre Timbaud) are the beating heart of the 11th *arrondissement* and the most *bobo* area of the capital, with open-air parties until late into the night.

SoPi, an abbreviation of South Pigalle, is the area to the south of the Boulevard de Rochechouart. Somewhat neglected until recently, it has found a new lease of life thanks to its cocktail bars and nightclubs.

Top tip: Fancy a late-night dip looking up at the stars in the middle of the Seine? Swing by the Joséphine Baker Pool in the capital's most futuristic neighborhood.

The Paris Métro does not run all night. There are trains until 1.15 A.M. from Sunday to Thursday, and until 2.15 A.M. on Fridays and Saturdays, so keep track of time, or you will have to make do with a night bus (the Noctilien service) or a cab.

Romantic Paris

Paris is famously the city of love, but also of sex and betrayal. And indeed why not? It all depends on the circumstances, after all, but a stolen kiss in Montmartre or a night of love among the rooftops of Paris are undoubtedly more scenic than anywhere else.

Tête-à-tête. You are enjoying an evening stroll across the Pont Neuf. Take your partner by the hand and walk down the flight of steps by the equestrian statue of Henri IV. At the tip of the Île de la Cité is a terrace overlooking the Seine, the heart of Paris. Now it is over to you.

Mur des Je t'aime (The Wall of Love). See 311 renderings of "I love you" in more than 250 languages on an enormous blue wall (Square Jehan-Rictus). Find the phrase in your partner's native tongue and declare your devotion.

In touch with your inner poet? In the gardens of the Palais Royal are eighteen benches, each with a poetic quotation. Select the one that means the most to you and your partner, and let nature take its course.

The most romantic park in Paris. The Musée Albert-Kahn (Albert-Kahn Museum) is located at the very gates of the capital, and here you will find Japanese, French, and English gardens, along with a forest and a meadow. It is an intimate and stunning space.

Futurist Paris

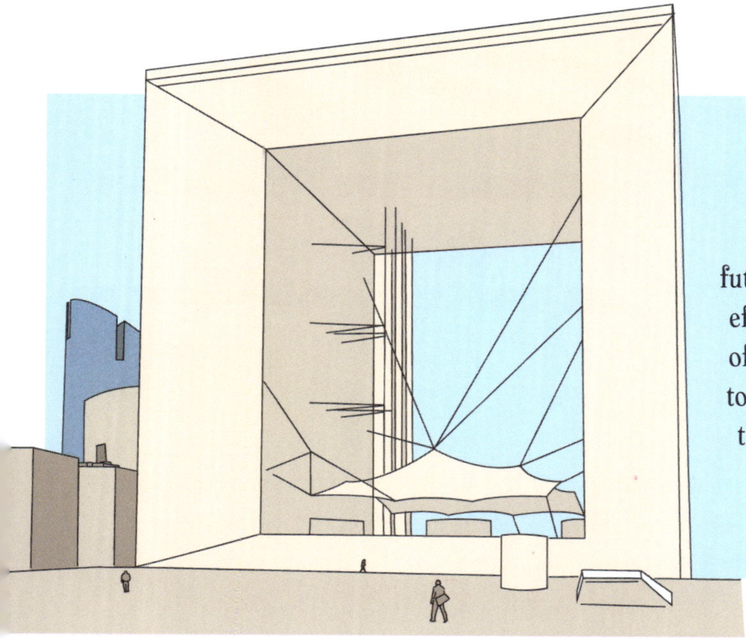

Despite its timeless, ancient charms, Paris has always had one eye to the future, and the subsequently disorienting effects have drawn criticism from some of its inhabitants. From the Eiffel Tower to its new and futuristic neighborhoods, the French capital has never ceased to reinvent itself.

La Défense. Complementing its towering skyscrapers and the Grande Arche (which rounds off a skyline that also features the Arc du Carrousel and the Arc de Triomphe), this business district is also an open-air museum crammed with high-profile sculptures, from Joan Miró's *Two Fantastic Characters* to Alexander Calder's *Red Spider*.

Paris Rive Gauche. The Bibliothèque nationale (National Library), the Cité de la Mode, the Passerelle Simone-de-Beauvoir footbridge, and a former hangar for refrigerated railcars that has been transformed into a cluster of artists' studios are just some of the treasures to be found in this up-and-coming area of Paris.

The **Philharmonie de Paris**, the home of the Paris Philharmonic, is a monumental creation by superstar architect Jean Nouvel. Its bold curves featuring a mosaic of some 265,000 aluminum birds look out over the city from the music complex.

Niemeyer's dome. This Modernist masterpiece atop the main meeting hall at the headquarters of France's Communist Party has naturally beguiled the world of fashion, from Prada to Jean Paul Gaultier.

Exotic Paris

Like many other large metropolises, Paris is a multicultural city in which ethnicities and religions from around the world coexist, finding their own niche within the fabric of the city, making it all the richer and more fascinating.

Africa in Paris. The La Chapelle metro station is the epicenter of the unique Goutte d'Or (Drop of Gold), a cosmopolitan neighborhood of chaotic thoroughfares, street markets, and ethnic restaurants.

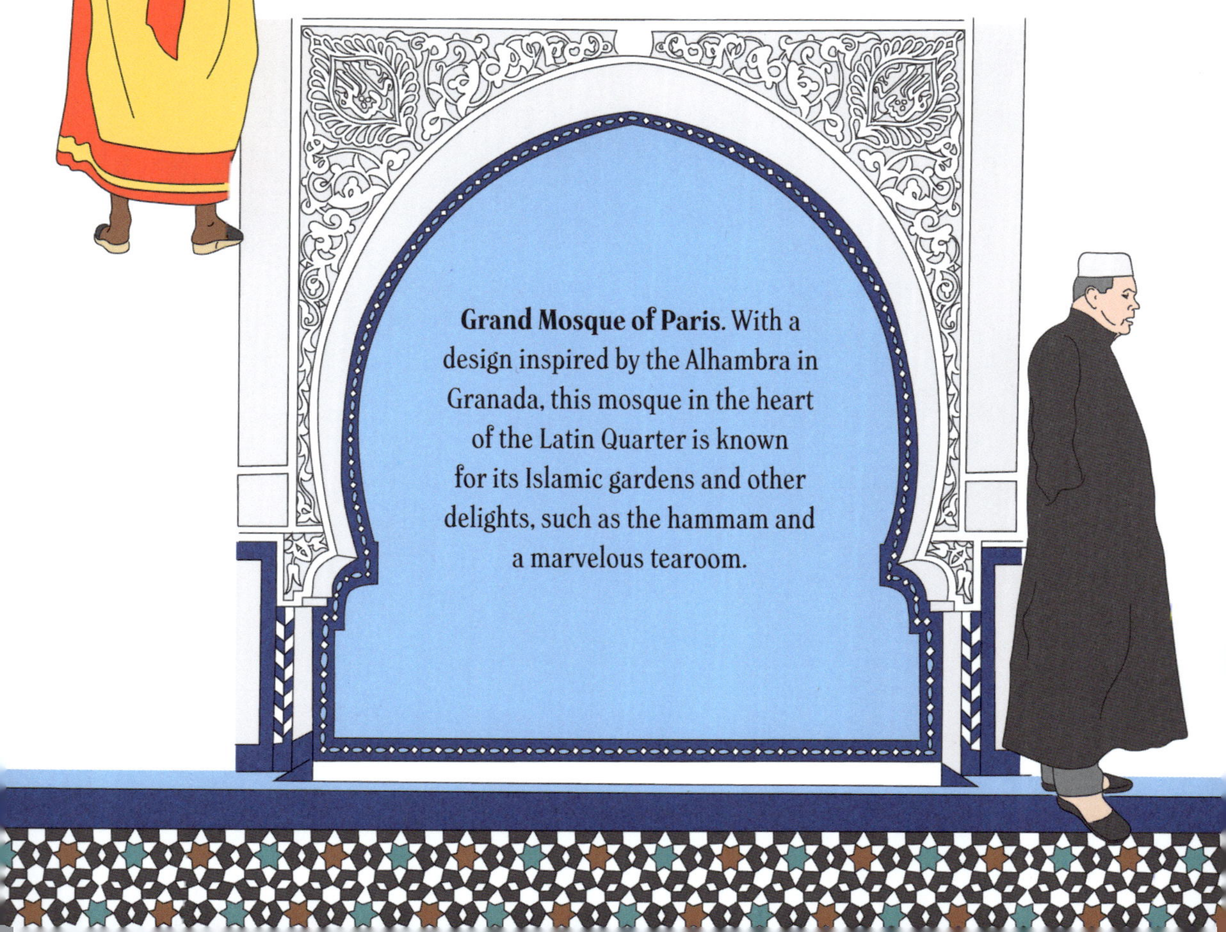

Grand Mosque of Paris. With a design inspired by the Alhambra in Granada, this mosque in the heart of the Latin Quarter is known for its Islamic gardens and other delights, such as the hammam and a marvelous tearoom.

Rue du Faubourg Saint-Denis. This bustling thoroughfare is one of the most multicultural streets in the city. The first part, closer to the Porte Saint-Denis, is lined with Turkish and Kurdish restaurants (try the Urfa Dürüm wrap!), while the other half is home to Indian restaurants.

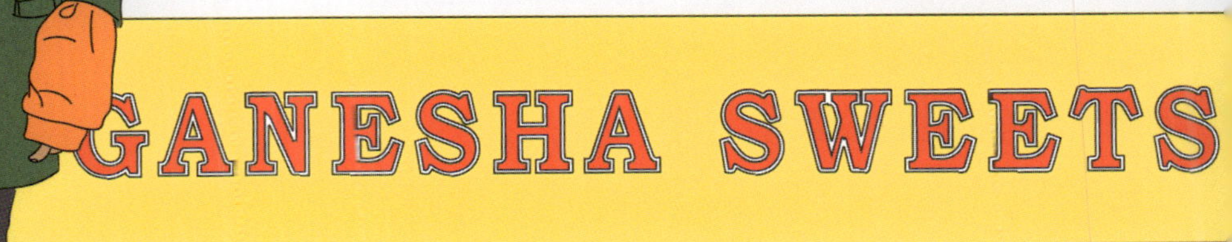

Little Tokyo. Japanophiles should check out the rue Sainte-Anne and the streets nearby, home to the finest ramen in Paris, along with a host of boutiques, bookstores, and confectioners, all bathed in the light of the Land of the Rising Sun.

Underground Paris

Paris is not just synonymous with elegance and romanticism. In the shadows of its splendid boulevards is a darker soul of rock and alternative sounds that is rarely mentioned but very familiar to Parisians rather than tourists.

Paris Est. The rock record stores in the 11th *arrondissement*, Belleville and its squats, street art, LSD, and running battles between punks and rockers, the dealers in Buttes-Chaumont park: while these areas are nothing like they were in the 1980s, traces of their underground past can still be seen.

Berlin in Paris. Fort d'Aubervilliers, an abandoned redoubt on the outskirts of Paris, now hosts art studios, bunkers, and alternative events in an artistic and cultural space to rival Berlin's underground aesthetic.

La Ferme du Bonheur. On a patch of land in Nanterre sandwiched between two highways, a prison, and an oil depot, you will find a "new hippie" farm on which pigs and sheep rub shoulders with fans of electronic music.

Vernon Subutex, the protagonist of punk writer Virginie Despentes's bestselling novel, has become the symbol of the Paris underground scene of the 1980s and '90s.

Instagrammable Paris

Paris makes it so easy to take great selfies with its huge array of iconic places and monuments. Here's a small selection of the more unusual and overlooked ones.

Place des Vosges. One of the most photogenic squares in Paris, with porticos, a geometric garden, and red-brick houses. It is the heart of Le Marais.

Square Rapp. One of the best vantage points to snap the Eiffel Tower.

Maison Loo. An enormous Chinese pagoda situated between classic Haussmann apartment buildings.

La Maison Rose. A charming small house high on the hill in Montmartre that was once a hangout for the artist friends of one of Picasso's wives.

Notre-Dame du Val-de-Grâce. An extravagantly Baroque church in the heart of the Latin Quarter.

Rue Crémieux is a pedestrianized street in the 12th *arrondissement*, famous for its small, very Parisian, and yet (weirdly) colorful houses.

Medici Fountain. One of the most beautiful corners of the Jardin du Luxembourg.

ARRÊTE! C'EST ICI L'EMPIRE DE LA MORT

The catacombs

These tunnels excavated into the limestone beneath Paris, once used as a cemetery, were transformed in 1809 to become an unusual (and somewhat macabre) museum beloved of tourists and those seeking out-of-the ordinary experiences.

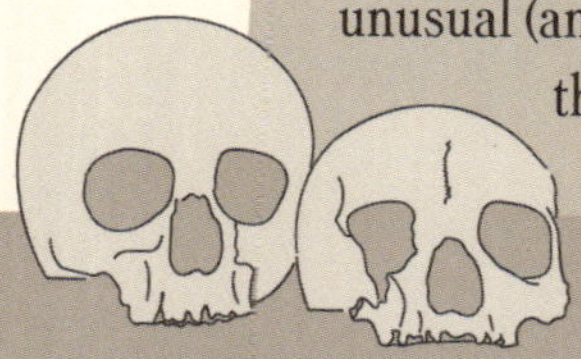

Underground mushrooms. Use of the capital's subterranean areas was kickstarted by the need to cultivate mushrooms, which was all the rage under Louis XIV. By the end of the nineteenth century, about a thousand tons of mushrooms were being produced every day.

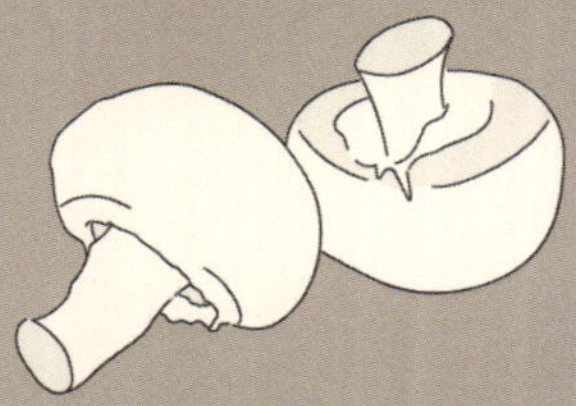

The *cataphiles*. In addition to the mile or so (2 km) of tunnels officially open to visitors, there are a further 215 miles (350 km) that some have dared to explore clandestinely. A veritable parallel life goes on down there, complete with dedicated rooms for parties and gigs.

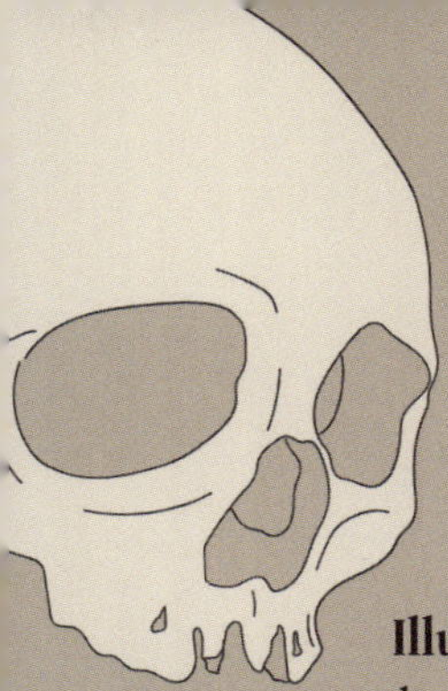

Illustrious corpses. The catacombs of Paris are also the last resting place of some celebrity remains, from the writers Rabelais, La Fontaine, and Perrault to the revolutionaries Robespierre and Danton.

Subterranean art. The catacombs have now become a bizarre subterranean museum. In addition to theatrical displays of skulls and bones, there are also some truly complex sculptures, including a reproduction of the fortifications in Port Mahon on the island of Menorca.

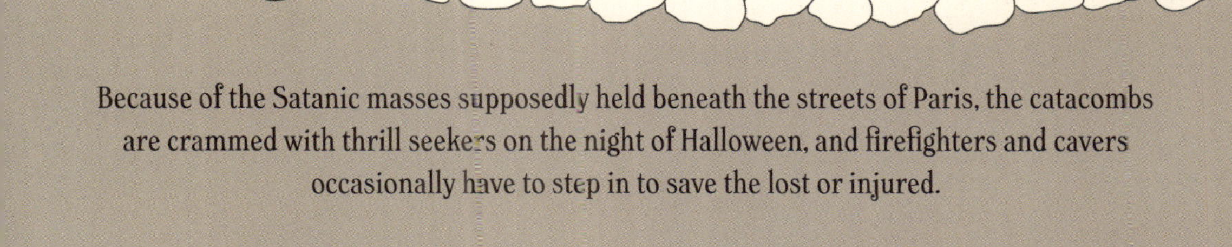

Because of the Satanic masses supposedly held beneath the streets of Paris, the catacombs are crammed with thrill seekers on the night of Halloween, and firefighters and cavers occasionally have to step in to save the lost or injured.

La Petite Ceinture

Before the trams, this railroad ring circling Paris connected the capital's main stations. The line was closed in 1993, and since then the various stretches of track and the disused stations have been opened to the public in stages.

Underground aesthetic. Like many other abandoned urban spaces, the Little Belt has become a symbol of alternative Paris, with the old infrastructure converted into cultural and community hubs, a wealth of graffiti, and the charm of the natural world's attempts to reclaim the space.

The unusual **Jardins du Ruisseau** are located next to the railroad track in the 18th *arrondissement* and are a perfect example of a collectively managed garden space with hundreds of different plant species.

Le Hasard Ludique. A restaurant with an outside terrace overlooking the track, a sculptor's studio, and a 250-seater concert venue all demonstrate what can be made of an old and abandoned station.

Workers of the world, unite! The TLM is an old railroad hall converted into a new kind of community space in which workers re-entering the workforce recycle textiles and cook alternative food at giveaway prices.

The countryside in Paris

A cluster of quiet byways lined with charming small villas only a stone's throw from the chaos and tower blocks of the 20th *arrondissement*, this little corner of the countryside in the heart of the metropolis will always be an unmissable if rather surreal exception to the essentially Parisian rule.

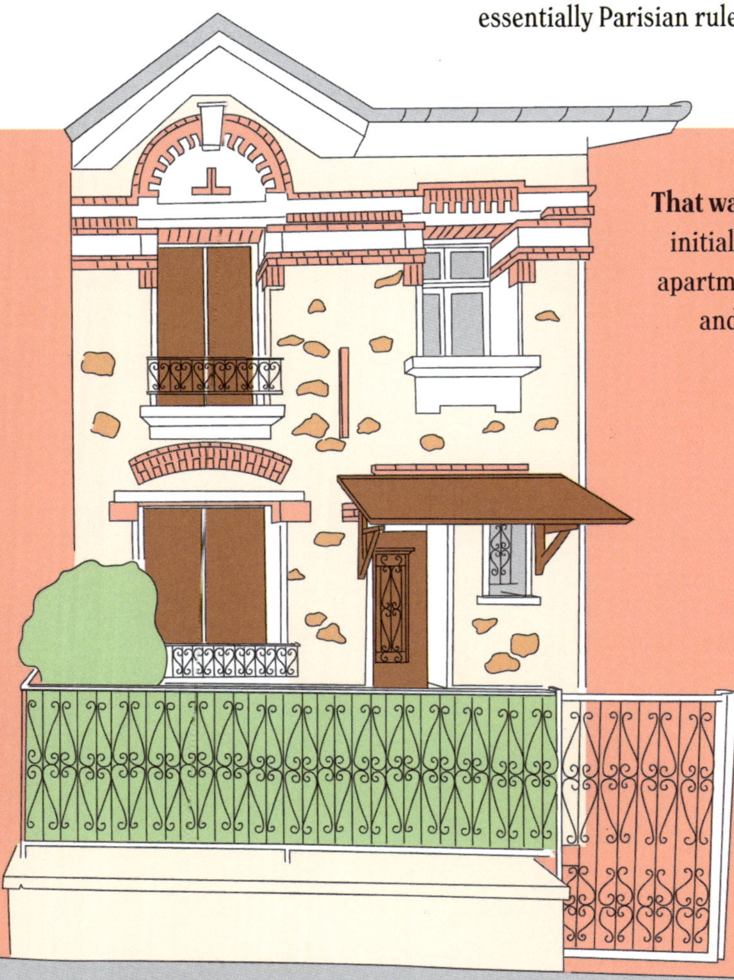

That was then, but this is now. The area was initially designed as a workers' village but apartments are now prohibitively expensive and the preserve of a privileged few.

It's no coincidence that François Hollande, ex-President of the Republic, has settled here.

Alternative architecture. There are no Haussmann-style mansion blocks here but instead the houses are low structures of brick or stone, with gabled roofs of Anglo-Norman or Alsatian inspiration.

Rue Saint-Blaise. With its cobblestones, café terraces packed with leisurely patrons, and a medieval bell tower at its far end (the church of Saint-Germain de Charonne), this small street in the heart of the village of Charonne is more like the main street of a country village.

Boulevard des Légendes. Moments from the peace and quiet of the area lies the chaos of Boulevard Mortier and, at no.141, the headquarters of France's secret service, made famous by the Canal+ series *Le Bureau des Légendes* (broadcast in English as *The Bureau*).

La Coulée Verte

The green pathway—a leafy walkway in the heart of the 12th *arrondissement*, extends 3 miles (5 km) from the Bastille to the Bois de Vincennes. It is not widely known but is dramatic and scenic.

Le Viaduc des Arts. The old railroad viaduct has now been pedestrianized and forms an elevated section of the walk from which you can inspect the facades of the neighboring building from a different perspective. The name comes from the art dealerships housed in the viaduct's arches.

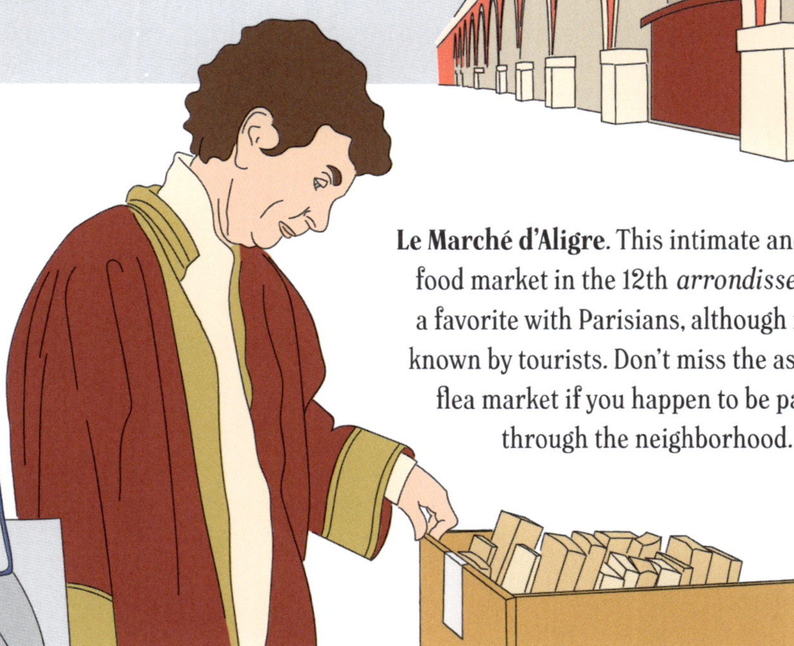

Le Marché d'Aligre. This intimate and friendly food market in the 12th *arrondissement* is a favorite with Parisians, although not well known by tourists. Don't miss the associated flea market if you happen to be passing through the neighborhood.

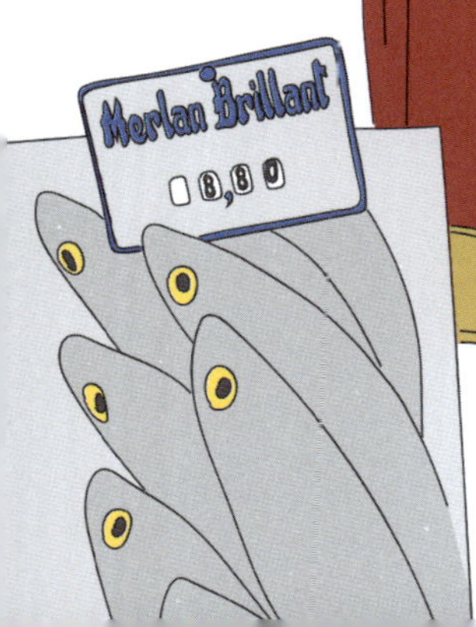

The **Jardin de Reuilly** is the largest of the four gardens along the pathway. You can cross from one side to the other via a bridge suspended over its 3¼ acres (1.5 hectares) of grassland.

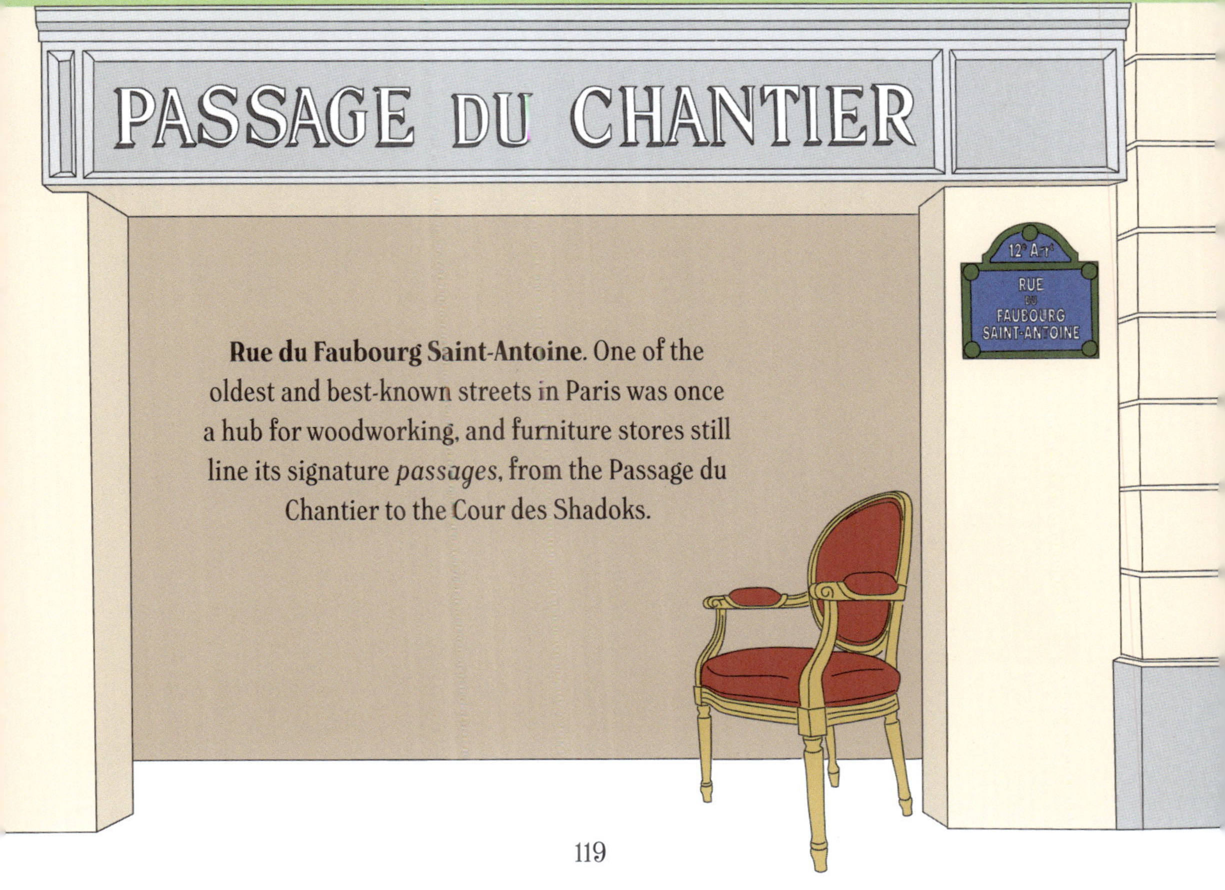

Rue du Faubourg Saint-Antoine. One of the oldest and best-known streets in Paris was once a hub for woodworking, and furniture stores still line its signature *passages*, from the Passage du Chantier to the Cour des Shadoks.

New Athens

This neighborhood located between Montmartre, the Paris Opera, and the Grands Boulevards area is somewhat overlooked by Parisians and tourists alike, but it promises authentic glimpses of a city with a glorious artistic past.

Notre-Dame-de-Lorette. This Neoclassical masterpiece epitomizes the strict formal architectural rules typical of the area, with a Greek-style facade and an Italianate interior inspired by Roman basilicas in particular.

Lorette was also the nickname given to ladies of easy virtue who frequented the area in the **mid-nineteenth century in search** of rich and powerful men to seduce.

Square d'Orléans. This small residential enclave is reminiscent of a London square and has been home to George Sand, Frédéric Chopin, and Alexandre Dumas, along with a host of other painters, sculptors, singers, and dancers.

Rue Victor Massé. This street is now best known for its incredible concentration of music stores, but it was once both home to Van Gogh (and his brother Theo) and the site of the famous Cotton Club, much beloved of Édith Piaf and Simone de Beauvoir in the same splendid mansion block at no.25.

Celebrities. The entrance to avenue Frochot stands beside a magnificent Art Deco window but is (sadly) blocked off by a gate. The street has been home to a host of luminaries, including Alexandre Dumas, Victor Hugo, Henri de Toulouse-Lautrec, Edgar Degas, and even the jazz guitarist Django Reinhardt.

Canal de l'Ourcq

This man-made canal is 80 miles (130 km) long and 200 years old. Its post-industrial feel has made it a symbol of eastern Paris and down-to-earth, Berlin-style alternative living.

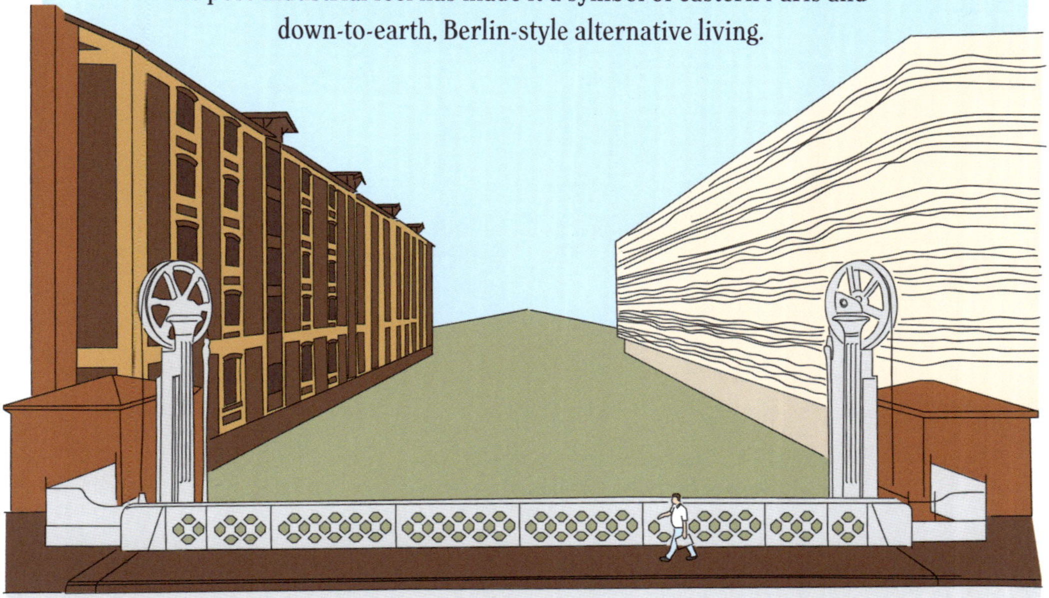

The **rue de Crimée lift bridge**, one of the few to be built entirely of metal rather than wood, was considered a technological marvel at the end of the nineteenth century.

The post-industrial **Grands Moulins de Pantin** overlooking the canal are now office buildings, but they were once working mills producing more than 200,000 tons of flour every year.

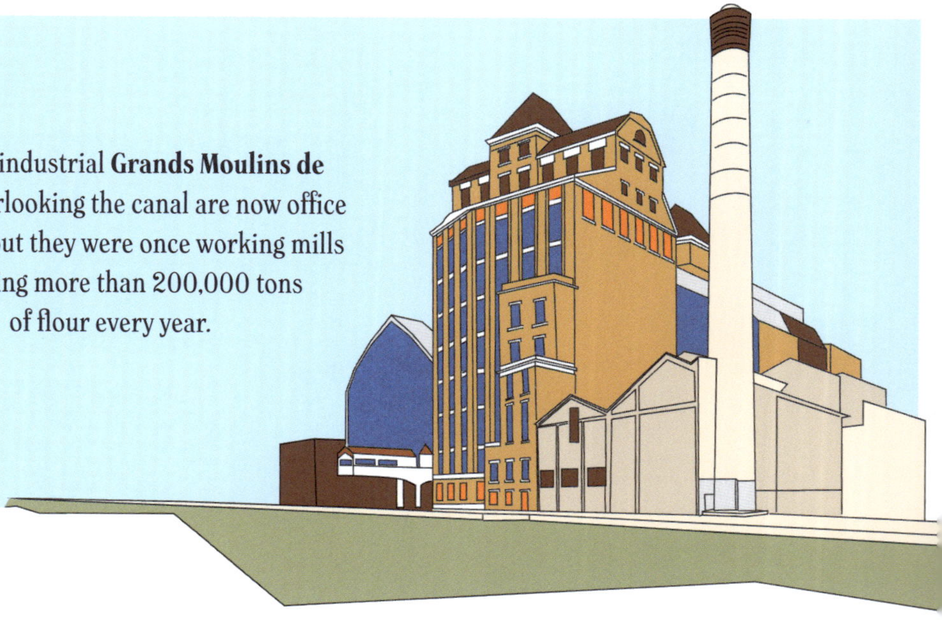

Marché sur l'eau. There is nothing like this alternative market anywhere else in Paris. You can buy produce grown near the city (Seine-et-Marne) and shipped along the canal to Pantin and the center in special barges. You would be hard-pressed to find food with fewer food miles!

MARCHÉ SUR L'EAU

Les Ourcq polaires. For the last few years, a group of Parisians have been getting together in Pantin three times a week to take a (freezing cold) dip in the canal, a practice that may be illegal but is becoming increasingly popular among extreme health enthusiasts.

Le Pavillon des Canaux. Try not to miss this canal-side multifunction venue. You can visit an exhibition, enjoy a drink, attend a drawing class, or go to a gig.

Visiting Paris with children

It's no secret that families with children tend to leave Paris and move out to the suburbs or the provinces because of the high prices and the claustrophobic apartments, but there is actually quite a lot on offer in the capital for little ones.

Ferme de Paris. This 12-acre (5-hectare) farm, with no entrance charge, is located in the Bois de Vincennes, not far from the eponymous racecourse (another exceptional place for young animal lovers).

Le Double Fond. A typical Parisian café-theater and an ideal place for children of all ages with an interest in magic tricks. On which note, it is also worth checking out the Musée de l'Illusion (Museum of Illusions), an interactive museum that is perfect for kids.

Les Pavillons de Bercy

Musée des Arts Forains (Fairground Museum). A world of dreams straddling tradition and modernity, and a must-see for the kids, who will undoubtedly be entranced by the charms of the most beautiful fairground rides in Europe and the unique atmosphere of the Pavillons de Bercy.

Jazz and snacks. Every Sunday afternoon, the doors of the legendary Sunset Sunside club open for jazz sessions designed especially for children, with snacks thrown in. It doesn't get more Parisian than this!

Visiting Paris with animals

According to a recent study, Paris is the most pet-friendly city in Europe, thanks to restaurants that often welcome them with open arms, the number of vets, and the quality of its green spaces.

Dog-friendly. Four-legged friends generally get a warm reception in Paris, especially on the small terraces typically found in front of bars and brasseries.

It is fairly common for waiters to provide a suitable bowl for your dog when seating you at a table.

Café des Chats. This restaurant and tearoom in the heart of the 11th *arrondissement* is famous for the presence of at least a dozen cats, which have been living there since 2013. Your own pet would naturally be welcome, too.

Le Caniparc Denfert Rochereau. The capital's first playground for animals is a space where you can let your dog off the leash (normally prohibited in most green spaces in the city).

ALPHA Dogs' House

Alpha Dogs' House. A three-story concept store dedicated to animal welfare, with a dog crèche, cat hotel, spa, and pet boutique.

A few stats. According to the city authorities, there are about 100,000 dogs and 250,000 cats in Paris, along with a Noah's Ark of more exotic pets, from rabbits to ferrets—as well as turtles and snakes, some of which are occasionally abandoned and risk ending up in the Seine.

From the Tour Montparnasse

One of the most impressive views of Paris is from 59 stories up on the rooftop of the Tour Montparnasse, although this magic is principally due to the fact that it is one of the few places where the rather architecturally ugly "sad tower" itself is not visible.

The Tour Montparnasse is the tallest skyscraper in Paris—689 ft (210 m) tall. It was the tallest building in Europe for seventeen years (until the Messeturm was built in Frankfurt in 1990). The tower and the observatory at the top will be closed for several years during renovation (from April 2026).

In a hurry to see Paris from above? The Tour Montparnasse boasts one of the fastest elevators in the world, capable of reaching the restaurant with its panoramic views on the 56th floor—643 ft (196 m) in the air—in just 38 seconds.

Skating with the stars. What was once the highest ice rink in Europe was located on the rooftop of the 59th floor and offered a unique and unmissable experience. Sadly, the ice rink closed in 2022.

The Tour Montparnasse looms over the eponymous railroad station that connects Paris to the Brittany region of France, so if you happen to find yourself passing through the neighborhood, you must try the best Breton *galettes* (savory pancakes) in the capital (in rue du Montparnasse and rue d'Odessa).

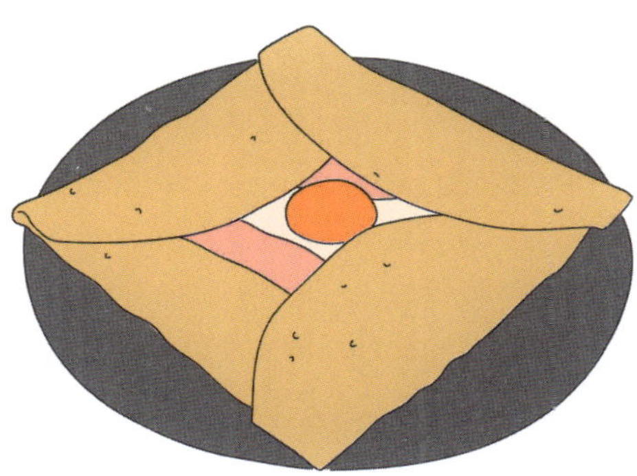

From the Sacré-Cœur

The most famous flights of steps in Paris, located on the most famous hill in Paris, will take you to the immaculate basilica of Sacré-Cœur in Montmartre. Try to take in the 360-degree panorama from the immense balcony looking out over the city.

The center of the world for art. The poorest artists started to live here in the first half of the **nineteenth** century as Montmartre was less expensive than the rest of the city, and the views painted on the slopes of that hill have taken their place in art history.

Why is the Sacré-Cœur always so white? When it comes into contact with water, the natural outer layer that protects the special kind of stone used to make the basilica produces a white substance that hardens in the sun. The Sacré-Cœur sports a new, pearly-white smile with every downpour!

The **Bateau-Lavoir**. Once a workshop and rendezvous for countless artists, from Cocteau, Apollinaire, and Modigliani to Picasso, who revolutionized painting by creating his *Les Demoiselles d'Avignon* here, one of the symbols of the area's artistic life.

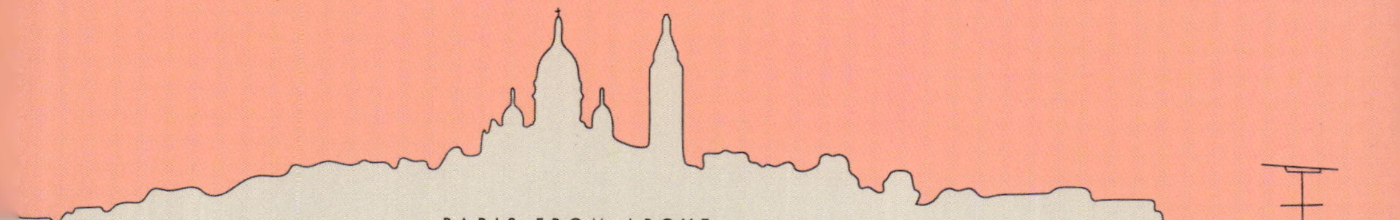

From the Butte Bergeyre

Most people are unaware of this hill in the heart of the 19th *arrondissement* with its small village, surrounded by the metropolis, from which there is a beautiful view of the neighboring hill of Montmartre and the Sacré-Cœur, especially at sunset.

In keeping with its rural style, there are few stores or cars on the Butte Bergeyre but instead cobbled streets, houses from the first half of **the twentieth century, a host** of community gardens, and a vineyard. Why not bring a sandwich?

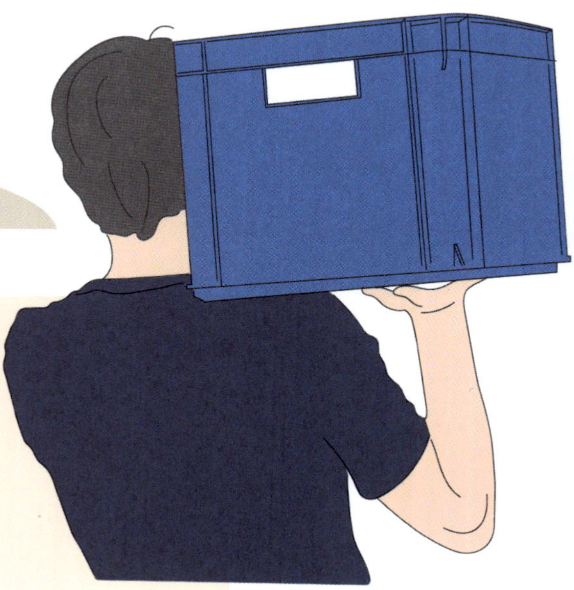

The secret vineyard. Tucked away in a community garden on the side of the hill, you will find 240 vines with a great view of Sacré-Cœur. They yield a few dozen bottles of rosé every year, 100 percent organic, 100 percent Parisian.

Fun fact (1): Every householder has the right to 10 square ft (**1 square m) of land** for cultivation, which explains why there are so many green-thumbed residents.

La Mouzaïa. You will find this odd little neighborhood just around the corner from the Butte Bergeyre and Buttes Chaumont Park, a labyrinth of "villas," narrow pedestrianized alleys lined with houses with gardens.

Fun fact (2): The French writer Henri Calet wrote his first novel *La Belle Lurette (A Long Time Ago)* in the neighborhood, the Italian socialist Pietro Nenni lived here from 1931 until 1940, and the French photographer Willy Ronis immortalized one of the three flights of steps leading up to the *butte* in a famous image.

Other unmissable bird's-eye views

1) From the Centre Pompidou (Pompidou Center). Designed by Renzo Piano and Richard Rogers and located in the heart of the capital. The view from the top floor, which you can access for free, is my favorite by far. The Pompidou Centre is now closed until 2030.

2) From the Parc de Belleville. One of the most beautiful views of Paris is from the Belvédère in this hilly park gracing a picturesque part of Paris 355 ft (108 m) above sea level: romantic and alternative.

3) From the Arc de Triomphe. Standing as the triumphant culmination of the Champs-Élysées and the centerpiece of the sprawling Place de l'Étoile, this monument has become an icon of the city. Its viewing terrace, some 165 ft (50 m) in the air, offers an alternative perspective on Paris and its impressive urban geometry.

4) From the Panthéon. The monumental palace of the Panthéon stands proudly in the Latin Quarter, the last resting place of the nation's great men and home to Foucault's legendary pendulum. The dome is open to visitors and boasts a breathtaking 360-degree panorama of the city.

On the trail of Princess Diana

Paris has a sad link to the tragic end of the life of Diana Spencer. On August 31, 1997 the people's princess died in a car accident in the Pont de l'Alma underpass while trying to escape from paparazzi who had taken an interest in her relationship with Dodi Fayed, an Egyptian businessman.

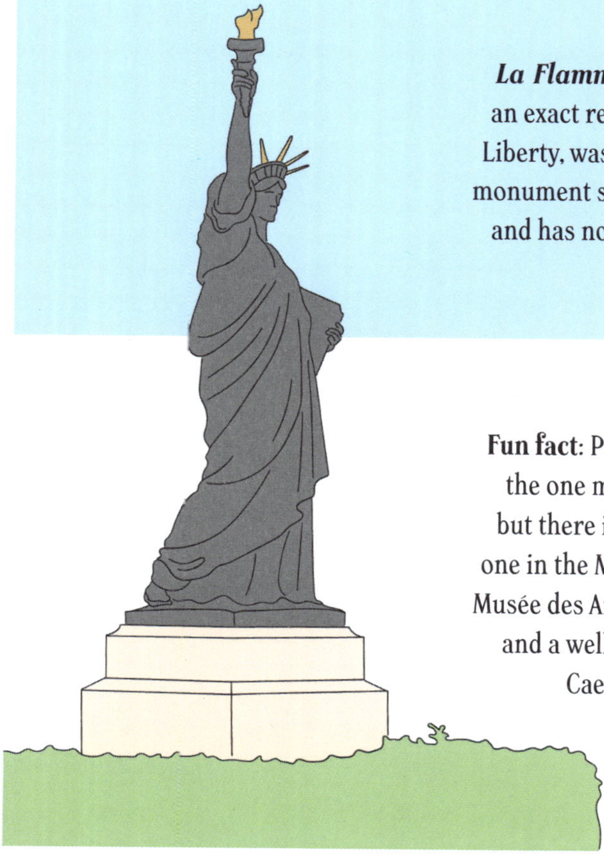

La Flamme de la Liberté. *The Flame of Liberty*, an exact replica of the flame of New York's Statue of Liberty, was given to France by the United States. The monument stands at the entrance to the Pont de l'Alma and has now become a memorial to Princess Diana.

Fun fact: Paris actually has six Statues of Liberty—the one mentioned here is on the Île aux Cygnes, but there is another in the Jardin du Luxembourg, one in the Musée d'Orsay (Orsay Museum), two in the Musée des Arts et Métiers (Industrial Design Museum), and a well-hidden one tucked into the Centaur of Caesar statue on Place Michel Debré.

The Ritz. Princess Diana stayed in this legendary hotel on the very elegant Place Vendôme during her final visit to Paris. This unique example of French-style luxury has been the gilded haunt of many celebrities, including Coco Chanel, Ernest Hemingway, Marcel Proust, and F. Scott Fitzgerald.

The French street artist 7Nuit has created a portrait of Princess Diana on the thirteenth pillar of the Alma tunnel, the exact scene of the accident (which is particularly difficult to reach), in homage to the princess.

Midnight in Paris

Woody Allen has always loved Europe, and Paris in particular, and Europe has loved him back, so much so that his movies are more successful in Europe than in the United States. *Midnight in Paris* is his magical and nostalgic tribute to the French capital.

Saint-Étienne-du-Mont. On the steps leading up to the northern door of this church just around the corner from the Panthéon, Gil, the movie's protagonist, finds himself catapulted back in time every evening, visiting the city's mythical artistic past.

Le Polidor. This restaurant in the heart of the Latin Quarter is one of the oldest in the city and was once a favorite haunt of Arthur Rimbaud and Paul Verlaine. Here, Gil meets the likes of Ernest Hemingway, from whom he seeks advice on writing his book.

Woody Allen's movie was inspired by Hemingway's book *A Moveable Feast*, in which the American writer describes the madness of his unforgettable years in Paris.

The Bristol. The parents of Gil's fiancée, Inez, are shown staying in the 3,400-square-foot (320-square-meter) penthouse suite of this luxury hotel, which boasts the largest private garden in the city, a swimming pool with a view of Sacré-Cœur, and even its own bakery.

Saturday Night Fever. Artists and intellectuals from all over the world would meet in the apartment of the feminist writer Gertrude Stein at the turn of the twentieth century, just as they do in the movie. They even used the correct address for filming, no.27, rue de Fleurus.

Amélie

This 2001 movie made by the then unknown French director and screenwriter Jean-Pierre Jeunet had the surprising side effect of revitalizing the image of Paris and the Montmartre area for a younger generation in particular.

Les Deux Moulins. This café and tobacconist's on the picturesque rue Lepic is where Amélie, the movie's protagonist, works as a waitress among other unforgettable and oddball characters. The café still exists, but it no longer sells cigarettes.

Collignon. The store run by the nasty greengrocer who unfairly torments his employee Lucien, is also still there. Au Marché de la Butte is located at no.56, rue des Trois Frères, on the first floor of the building in which Amélie lives.

Le Fabuleux Destin d'Amélie Poulain

Photo booth. These photo booths are a typical sight in Paris and are essential when filling out most forms to be submitted to the French authorities. They play a key role in the movie and Amélie's is located at no.53, rue des Trois Frères.

Au Clown de la République. Some might be surprised to learn that Parisians adore fancy dress parties. Amélie is no exception (although her motives are different in this case) and she finds everything she needs to dress up as Zorro in this historic store on boulevard Saint-Martin.

The Da Vinci Code

Dan Brown's bestselling novel and the subsequent movie adaptation with Tom Hanks still draw hordes of fans to certain locations in Paris, even though the American author's fascinating theories often tend to be pure fiction.

Saint-Sulpice. One of the largest churches in Paris, famed for its astronomical gnomon, a marble obelisk that can be used to calculate the spring equinox. In Dan Brown's novel, it is posited as the course of the so-called Rose Line, the prime meridian of the world.

The Inverted Pyramid. According to Dan Brown, this upside-down pyramid located beneath the enormous pyramid designed by architect I. M. Pei (which now serves as the entrance to the Louvre) marks the final location of the Holy Grail and the tomb of Mary Magdalene. A more likely story is that it is a skylight for the Carrousel du Louvre shopping mall.

Château de Villette. In Ron Howard's movie, this splendid manor house about half an hour outside Paris is owned by Sir Leigh Teabing, a historian and Holy Grail expert to whom the protagonists Robert Langdon and Sophie Neveu turn for help.

Château du Clos Lucé. If you are a Leonardo da Vinci fan, you will enjoy inspecting his greatest inventions in this château in the Loire Valley, a couple of hours outside Paris. Look out for a flying machine, an armored car, a helicopter, and a revolving bridge, among many things.

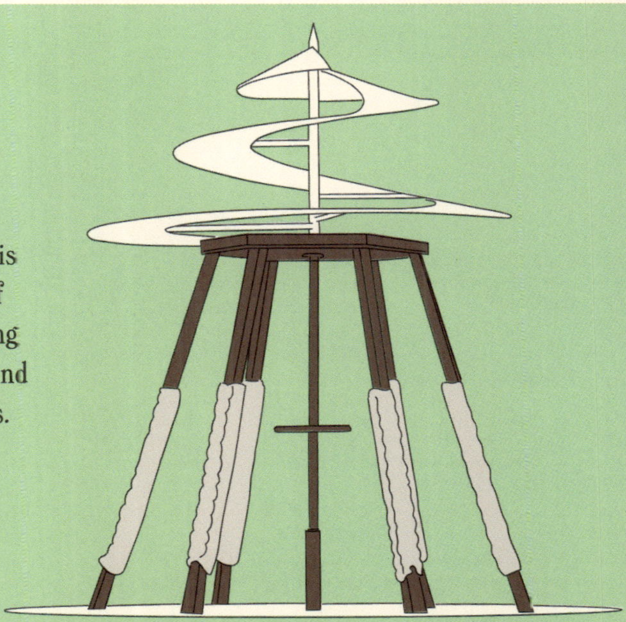

The Phantom of the Opera

Thanks to the many adaptations for stage and screen (not least Andrew Lloyd Webber's musical), Gaston Leroux's novel has exerted a powerful influence on the popular imagination and made the Palais Garnier in Paris a place of myth and legend.

Who is the phantom? The legend begins with a supposedly true story. There was indeed a fire at the Salle Le Peletier in 1873 and it was rumored to have cost a young ballerina her life. Legend has it that her disfigured fiancé, a pianist named Ernest, who managed to escape, fled to the basement of the Palais Garnier, which was being built at the time.

· ACADÉMIE · NATIONALE · DE · MUSIQUE ·

The Paris Opera. Paris's temple to ballet was designed by Charles Garnier, a young and practically unknown architect, and is a work of art in itself, the culmination of the unique view down the majestic avenue de l'Opéra.

Unlucky 13! During a performance of Gounod's *Faust* on May 20, 1896, the auditorium's enormous chandelier fell down into the audience, killing a patron. Legend has it that the victim was sitting in seat no.13. Was it all Ernest's doing?

A lake beneath the stage? The underground lake near where Ernest the phantom was supposed to live was actually real. There used to be a pool of groundwater (with a population of carp) that complicated construction of the Opera. It was eventually channeled into a concrete vat.

Last Tango in Paris

The older and despairing Marlon Brando, the young and unsettling Maria Schneider, an empty Parisian apartment: the ingredients of Bernardo Bertolucci's 1972 cult movie, which has seduced and scandalized multiple generations of viewers, are sparse but unforgettable.

Bertolucci and Paris. Together with the movie that immortalized him, the Italian director had also shot parts of his previous movie (*The Conformist*, from the novel by Alberto Moravia) in the French capital and, in 2003, went on to direct *The Dreamers*, which is set in the Paris of May '68.

That was then, but this is now. Paris has changed considerably since the 1970s, as evidenced by what is shown in the movie. The Tour Montparnasse was still being built at the time (these days, some want it demolished), the Musée d'Orsay was still a train station, and the place where some apartment buildings once stood beside the Canal Saint-Martin is now a park.

The apartment. The movie was shot almost in its entirety in a 1,300-square-ft (120-square-m) apartment on the seventh floor of a splendid apartment building on rue de l'Alboni.

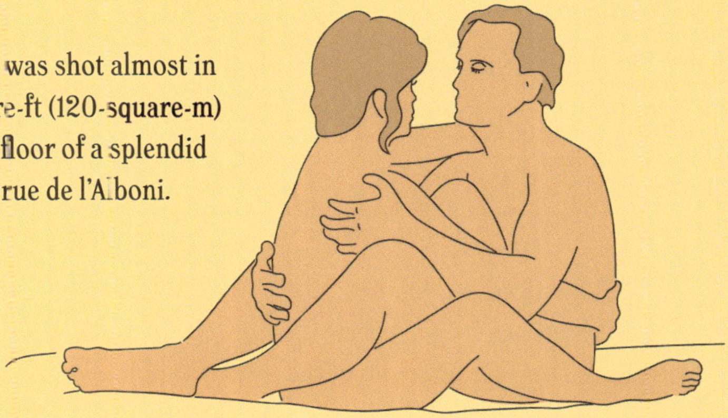

This extremely elegant thoroughfare in the 16th *arrondissement* leads directly to the Pont de Bir-Hakeim, the bridge where the lovers meet for the first time.

Salle Wagram. The final tango scene is set in the oldest ballroom in Paris, with 8,600 square ft (800 square m) of dance floor and a 40-ft (12-m) high ceiling. It has played host to everything from car shows to boxing matches over the years, and some of the biggest names in musical history have played here, from Herbert von Karajan to Duke Ellington, Maria Callas, and Bud Powell.

Rue des Eaux. This street, which is used as a location in Bertolucci's movie but also makes an appearance in other movies such as *The Professional* with Jean-Paul Belmondo, has a unique feature: after the first 425 ft (13 m), it turns into a narrow alley with a 200-ft (63-m) flight of steps, an (unexpected) taste of Montmartre in the heart of the 16th *arrondissement.*

Paris and the *Nouvelle Vague*

Truffaut, Godard, Varda, Rohmer ... the unforgettable scenes from their movies have ensured that the directors of the so-called *Nouvelle Vague* played a crucial role in reinventing the urban spaces of Paris, liberating them from hackneyed clichés and catapulting them into the modern age.

From the city as wallpaper to the city as character. For the *Nouvelle Vague*, Paris ceased to be merely a backdrop and became a protagonist in the plot, reflecting or influencing the characters' emotions. Suddenly, anything was possible, from cavorting on the roof of Le Châtelet to running at full tilt through the Louvre.

Bande à part (Band of Outsiders). In the most famous scene in Jean-Luc Godard's movie, Anna Karina, Sami Frey, and Claude Brasseur take up the challenge to run through the Louvre as quickly as possible. They managed a time of 9 minutes and 42 seconds, although their record was to be broken by Eva Green, Louis Garrel, and Michael Pitt in Bertolucci's movie *The Dreamers*.

Anna Karina. Godard's movies have turned the Franco-Danish actress into a living meme. Her monologue in the bar near Strasbourg-Saint-Denis (in *Une femme est une femme/A Woman is a Woman*) or the scene where she recites poetry by Louis Aragon at Liberté metro station (*Bande à part/Band of Outsiders*) are unforgettable.

Truffaut/Doinel. From his debut feature movie (*Les quatre cent coups/The 400 Blows*) onward, the French director has paid homage to the neighborhood in which he was born, around Clichy, Saint-Georges, and Pigalle. It is here that Antoine Doinel, his doppelgänger, lives out his adventures among ordinary (and oddball) characters who work in the bistros, stores, and hotels of Paris.

Ratatouille

The Aristocats, *The Hunchback of Notre-Dame*, *Anastasia*: many of Disney's animated classics are set in Paris, and a particularly memorable one is the story of Remy, the legendary rat chef, and his unusual journey through the universe of French cuisine (and the occasional American cliché).

The sewers of Paris. The headquarters of Remy's (in)famous colleagues living in the capital. There is also a real museum, the Musée des Égouts (Sewer Museum), which recently underwent major renovation work, that offers an alternative option for discovering Paris's underground levels.

La Tour d'Argent. The restaurant run by chef Auguste Gusteau, Remy's mentor, was obviously inspired by this historic institution in the 5th *arrondissement*, which is famous for its panoramic views of Notre-Dame and its signature version of *duck à l'orange*.

Pont au Double. The young and clumsy garbage boy Linguini tries to convince Remy to work for him in a scene beneath this metal bridge (one of the shortest in Paris), connecting the square in front of Notre-Dame and the left bank of the Seine.

Of Rats and Men. When Remy is wondering whether rats can trust humans, his father takes him to a store specializing in pest control. This is Aurouze, a historic (and photogenic) business that exists to this day, a stone's throw from Châtelet.

To bring their protagonists to life, the screenwriters took inspiration from people in real life. The talented and stubborn Colette is based on the famous chef Hélène Darroze, Auguste Gusteau is a cross between French chef Bernard Loiseau and the late French chef Paul Bocuse, and the food critic Anton Ego looks suspiciously like the French actor Louis Jouvet.

Daniel Pennac's Belleville

The French writer Daniel Pennac has (rightly) helped to put the multicultural neighborhoods of Belleville and Ménilmontant in eastern Paris on the map. In book after book the many and various adventures of the down-at-heel Malaussène clan are played out.

Le Zèbre de Belleville. Once a movie theater frequented by the Malaussène family, this is now a cabaret, circus, and gig venue. Weekend circus workshops are also organized for adults and children, embodying the festive and creative spirit of the area.

Ménilmontant. With its pedestrianized streets, graffiti, busy bars, chaotic feel, and multicultural, uplifting atmosphere, this hilly neighborhood next door to Belleville is a window on a unique side of Paris and one of the most authentic areas in the capital.

Hôpital Saint-Louis. Various characters in Pennac's novels enjoy temporary but regular stays in this hospital in the 10th *arrondissement*. It is also famous for housing a museum containing the world's largest collection of wax casts.

Rue de la Mare. In the 1987 novel *The Fairy Gunmother*, the dreadful architect Ponthard-Delmaire lives on rue de la Mare, which is also home to the footbridge over the Little Belt, immortalized by the French photographer Willy Ronis. The adjacent rue de Cascades inspired Yann Tiersen's eponymous instrumental album.

SUCHARD

Rue de la Folie-Régnault. The Malaussène family live at no.78 on this street in the 11th *arrondissement*. The area's typical red-brick houses were once the preserve of workers and artisans, and the Suchard chocolate factory was based here until the mid-1900s.

The Party

The comedy called *La Boum* that sent the career of Sophie Marceau into the stratosphere (she was later to become an icon of French cinema) is a carefully observed, if now slightly nostalgic, snapshot of 1980s Paris that captured the hearts of a generation.

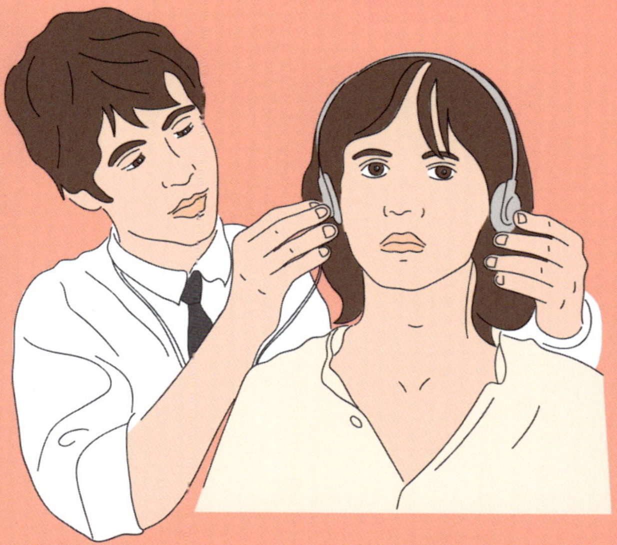

Lycée Henri-IV. The Latin Quarter is without doubt the main character in the movie. Vic, the protagonist, and her friends attend one of Paris's most prestigious public high schools, an institution renowned as the *alma mater* of many of the country's most celebrated intellectuals, politicians, and scientists.

We used to go to Le Corinto. Vic's parents' favorite "Italian" restaurant at no.237, rue du Faubourg Saint-Honoré is no longer there, and many other rather kitsch, pseudo-Italian places have fallen out of fashion in much the same way. Italian restaurants in Paris now tend to be genuinely Italian.

La Coupole

La Coupole. The brasserie where Vic and her legendary great-grandmother go for lunch is one of the most famous in Paris and an institution in the Montparnasse area (along with La Rotonde, around the corner), renowned for its Art Deco style and iconic decorated dome.

La Main Jaune (Yellow Hand). This was the first roller disco in France, opening in the 17th *arrondissement* after the roller-skating craze had blown up. Sadly for fans of the movie, it closed its doors in 2003, but reopened in spring 2026 as a creative hub with recording studios, a bar, restaurant, and a space for DJ sets.

Édith Piaf

Despite her frail physique and awkward manner, *la Môme Piaf* (Piaf, the Little Sparrow) carved out a niche for herself as one of the most powerful and unforgettable voices in history as she became France's ambassador to the world. Known as a "man-eater," with a fiery, brazen character, she lived life on a knife-edge between light and shadow.

Rags to riches. Édith Piaf was born in the working-class district of Belleville and abandoned by her mother in the direst of circumstances, but transcended her origins to live in dream houses like the private mansion on rue Leconte-de-Lisle, where she was sadly to grieve the premature death of the boxer Marcel Cerdan, one of her greatest loves.

Place Édith Piaf. This charming small square in the Gambetta district is not far from the Hôpital Tenon, the hospital in which Édith Piaf was born in 1915. An original bronze sculpture by Lisbeth Delisle stands at its center, immortalizing the Little Sparrow in a characteristic pose, her arms reaching up to the sky and her heart open to the world.

The apartment/museum. This small, two-room apartment in the 11th *arrondissement* (at no.5, rue Crespin du Gast), where the artist lived in 1933, has been turned into a museum crammed with items of interest, from her collection of stage shoes to excerpts from her private correspondence, and even a pair of boxing gloves once belonging to Cerdan.

The Olympia. Édith Piaf was a friend of Bruno Coquatrix, the venue's historic proprietor, and performed exclusively here for a two-month run in 1958 and three months in 1961, transforming it into the symbolic backdrop of her successful career. This Parisian music hall is famous to this day for displaying artists' names in illuminated block letters.

Coco Chanel

Gabrielle Chanel revolutionized fashion and turned Paris into a global symbol of elegance. Paradoxically, with her mother dead and her father having walked out, she owed the sober and austere style that immortalized her name to a childhood spent with her sisters at a convent orphanage in Corrèze, southwest France.

Place Vendôme. One of the most elegant squares in Paris is inextricably linked with the name of Coco Chanel, who resided continuously at the Ritz (in the suite that now bears her name) from 1937 until her death in 1971. The brand's recently renovated luxury jewelry store is now also located on the same square.

Rue Cambon. In 1910, Coco Chanel opened her first boutique (in which she sold her hats) at no.21 on this street, around the corner from Place Vendôme. Just a few years later, in 1927, the success of her fashion house would allow her to own five buildings on the street, from no.23 to no.31.

The Chanel building, floor by floor.
1st floor: boutique;
2nd floor: a room for presenting collections and fittings of *haute couture* dresses;
3rd floor: Coco Chanel's apartment;
4th floor: Coco Chanel's studio (where Karl Lagerfeld also worked);
attic: design workshop.

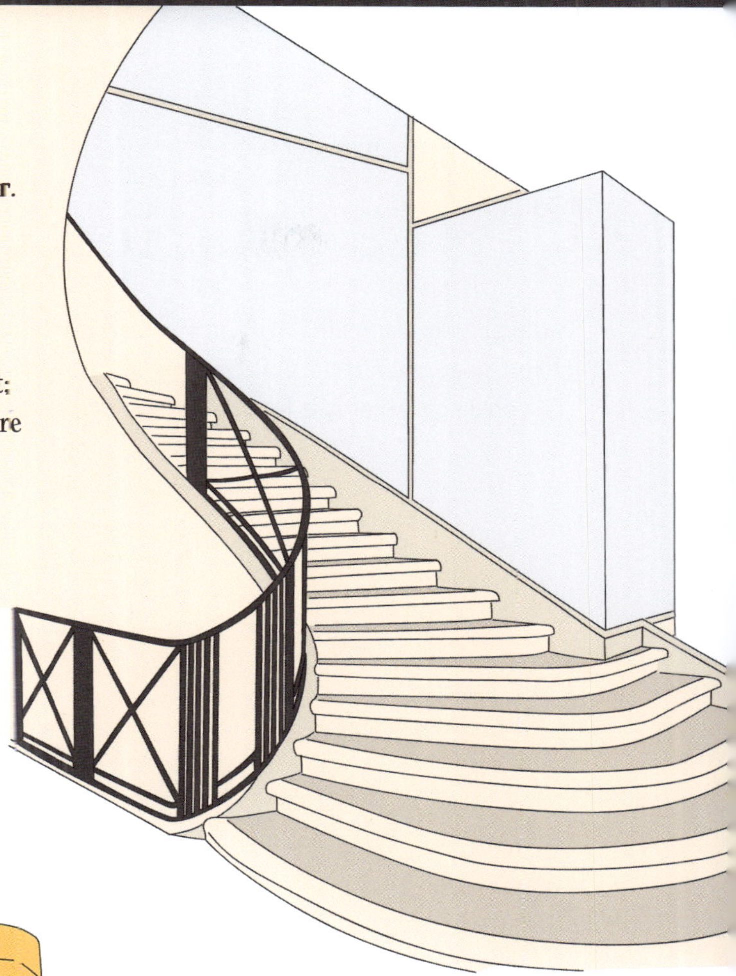

5 iconic creations:
1) The little black dress
2) The tailored tweed suit
3) Two-tone ballet flats
4) The 2.55 quilted bag
5) No.5 parfum

Fun fact: The bottle for the famous Chanel No.5 had been designed by her lover at the time, Grand Duke Dmitri Pavlovich, and was modeled on the vodka flasks used by the Russian Imperial Guard.

Marie Curie

Two-time Nobel laureate Marie Curie, whose surname at birth in Warsaw was Skłodowska, found fame and fortune in Paris, a city she had chosen for her studies and would never abandon, eventually becoming an incomparable model for a woman in science

Blazing a trail. Marie Curie was the first woman to hold a professorial chair at the Sorbonne, the first to head a laboratory, the first to be admitted to France's National Academy of Medicine, the first to be awarded a Nobel Prize—indeed, the only one to be awarded two (in Physics and Chemistry)—and the first to be buried in the Panthéon.

The first laboratory. Not long after she met Pierre Curie, her future husband, the two scientists began to work day and night in a shed on rue Lhomond in the 5th *arrondissement*, which was more like a cowshed than a scientific laboratory. It was here that they would discover radium, the chemical element that won them their first Nobel Prize.

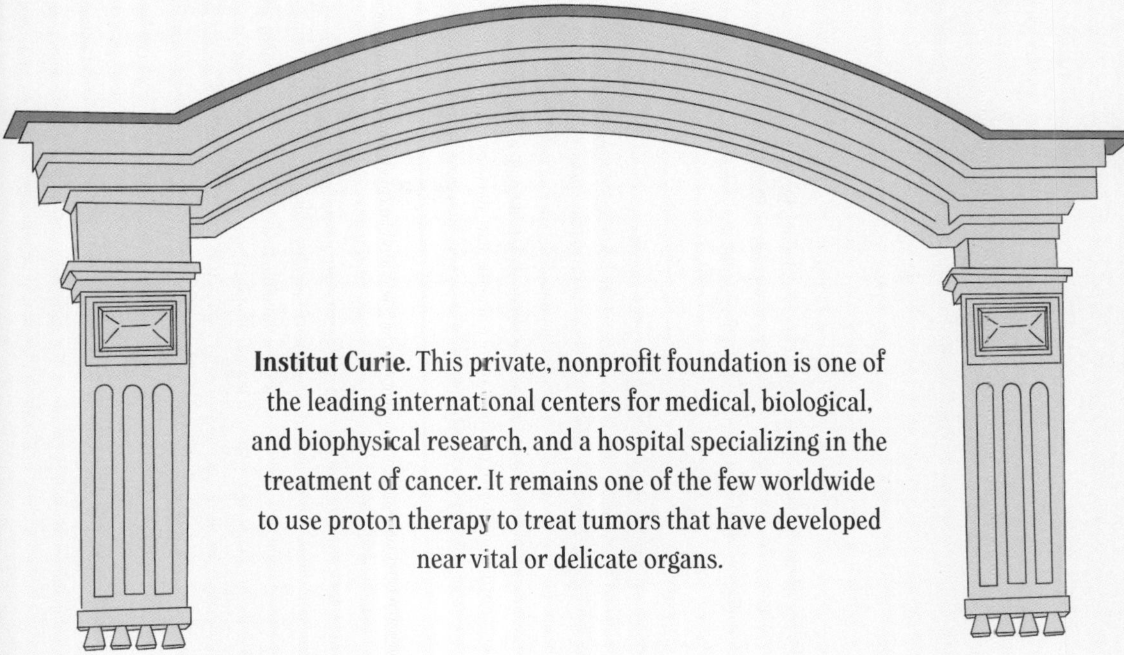

Institut Curie. This private, nonprofit foundation is one of the leading international centers for medical, biological, and biophysical research, and a hospital specializing in the treatment of cancer. It remains one of the few worldwide to use proton therapy to treat tumors that have developed near vital or delicate organs.

Musée Curie. The first floor of what was once the Institut du Radium (no.1, rue Pierre et Marie Curie) houses exhibits, photographs, and documents chronicling the history of radioactivity and the private life of the Curie family. You can also take a look at Marie Curie's old study and chemistry laboratory.

Fun fact. Because of Marie Curie's experiments involving radioactivity, her body, which is interred beneath the dome of the Panthéon, was buried in a coffin lined with a layer of lead 0.1 in (2.5 mm) thick.

Kiki de Montparnasse

Model, actress, ballerina, singer, and painter as the occasion demanded, the fiery and indomitable Alice Prin, nicknamed Kiki or the Queen of Montparnasse because of her life of straitened circumstances and intense, extravagant relationships, became one of the symbols of bohemian life in the Paris of the 1920s.

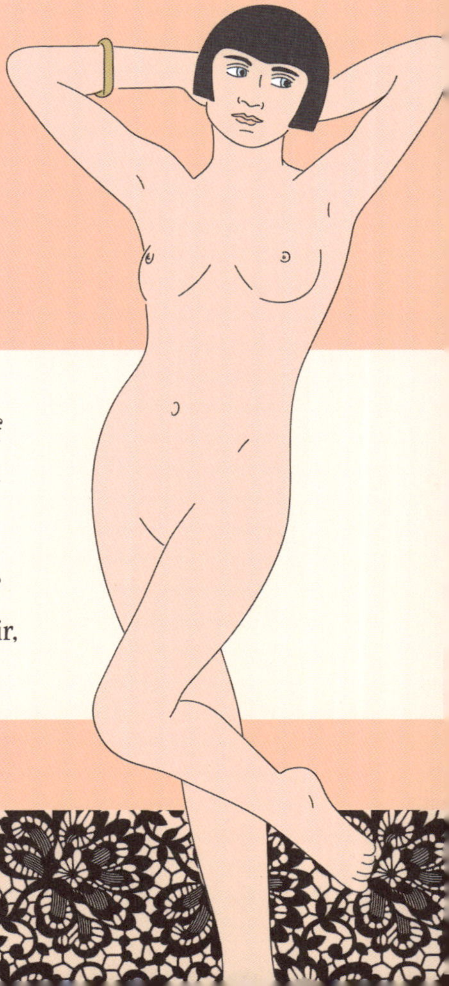

From Alice to Kiki. As an illegitimate daughter looked after by her grandmother until the age of twelve, Alice had always needed to be creative in finding ways to make ends meet until she began nude modeling after her arrival in Paris from Burgundy, posing for the most famous artists of the time and adopting her iconic style: bobbed hair, lipstick, and kohl-rimmed eyes. A star was born.

Le violon d'Ingres **(Ingres's violin).** Kiki was the muse and for six years the partner of the American photographer Man Ray, one of the greatest exponents of Dadaism and Surrealism. In his most famous and scandalous photo, Kiki poses naked and is snapped from behind, becoming a violin, and the female body becomes an instrument to be played.

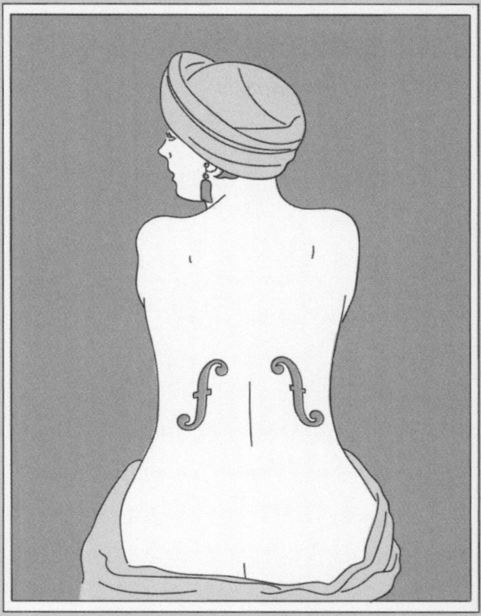

Carrefour Vavin. The junction of boulevard du Montparnasse and boulevard Raspail has been renamed Place Pablo Picasso in homage to the artists of the 1920s who were regular patrons of the neighborhood's now legendary establishments: La Rotonde, Le Dôme, La Coupole, and Le Select.

The life of an artist. Kiki and Man Ray lived together in a magnificent Art Deco building in the 14th *arrondissement* (no.31b, rue Campagne-Première) which was made up of artists' studios. It was here that the couple would rub shoulders with the greatest celebrities of the age, such as painters Pablo Picasso and Henri Matisse, writers André Breton and Paul Éluard, and many more.

Simone de Beauvoir

The story of this feminist, writer, and leading intellectual in French culture is intertwined with the Left Bank and the Saint-Germain and Montparnasse areas, where she lived, studied, and most importantly wrote the books that would forever change her era and revolutionize the lives of women.

Scandal at the Lycée Molière. Simone de Beauvoir taught at this high school in the 16th *arrondissement* from 1936 until 1939, but was sacked for having an affair with one of her pupils. After being suspended from teaching following a complaint that she incited a minor to depravity, she gave up the profession altogether.

Parisian cafés. Simone de Beauvoir was famously a tireless worker, hence her nickname *Castor* (beaver). She spent entire days writing in her favorite bars, mostly at Flore, but also at Le Dôme, La Closerie des Lilas, and Le Raspail Vert, both alone and in the company of her partner Jean-Paul Sartre.

La Closerie des Lilas

Le Cours Désir. The Catholic high school for girls in which de Beauvoir spent her adolescence is discussed from a slightly critical perspective in her 1958 autobiography *Memoirs of a Dutiful Daughter*. The site (no.35, rue Jacob) is now home to the Librairie des Femmes (Women's Bookshop), one of the bastions of feminist culture in Paris.

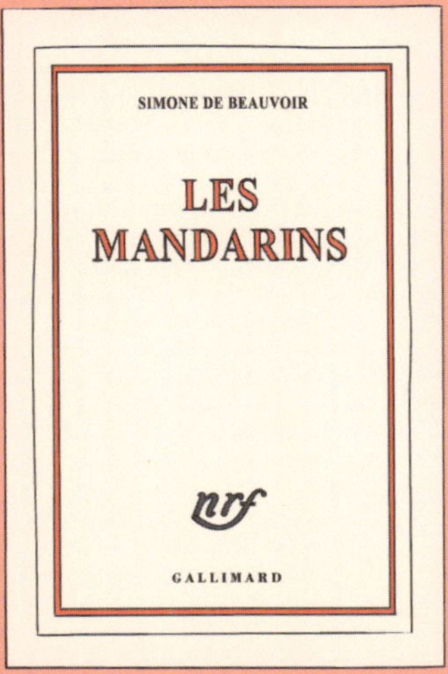

Quartier Générale. After winning the Prix Goncourt (France's premier literary prize) with *The Mandarins* (1954), Simone de Beauvoir bought her first apartment (at no.11b, rue Victor Schœlcher) and it was here that the famous *Manifesto of the 343* was drafted.

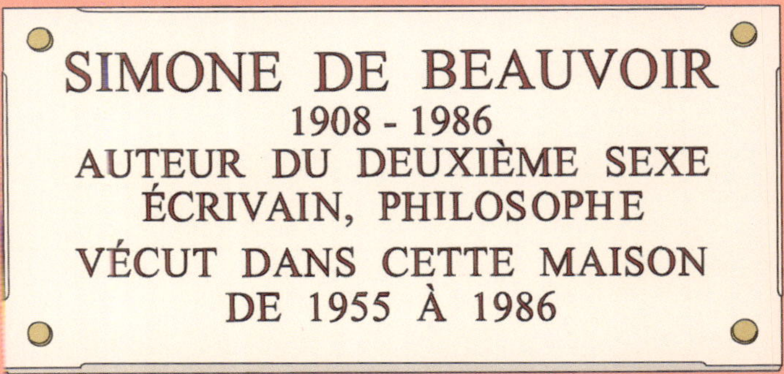

La Rhumerie. Simone de Beauvoir loved the nightlife, restaurants, and underground jazz clubs of Saint-Germain-des-Prés. This cocktail bar, still in business, was one of her favorite places to relax with friends after endless days of work.

Louise Michel

The so-called *vierge rouge* (red virgin) was a pioneer of the feminist movement, not to mention an anarchist, teacher, writer, and importantly an indefatigable revolutionary. She has become one of the most famous and revered female figures in French history.

The Paris Commune. The Commune was a historically unique experiment in direct democracy that lasted only seventy-two days, but these were enough to emblazon Louise Michel's derring-do in the memory of later generations. Dubbed the "bloodthirsty she-wolf" by the press, Louise took an active part in defending the Communards, both as a "soldier" and as a nurse.

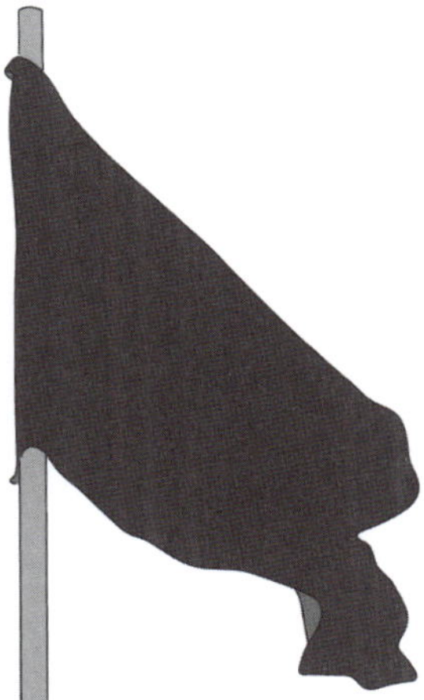

Red flag/black flag. After embracing anarchist thought during her exile in New Caledonia after the failure of the Commune, Louise Michel was the first to bring the black flag to Paris. From this moment on, it became the symbol of the anarchist movement, supplanting the red flag of libertarian socialism.

Square Louise Michel. Ironically, this enormous square with its network of steps ascending to the top of the Butte Montmartre bears the name of the heroine of the Commune, even though the Sacré-Cœur, which stands proudly above it, was specifically designed as the symbol of a "new moral order" intended to entomb that experience of revolution.

Fun fact. Only 11 of the **Paris Métro's** 302 stations are named after women and, of these, Louise Michel is the only one to have a station named after her alone, without having to share the honor with a husband or other man.

The *bouquinistes*

What would the Seine be without its *bouquinistes*? You'll find them all along the Right Bank. There are no fewer than 226 open-air bookstores, with 900 green metal display boxes crammed full of prints, postcards, and books both modern and antiquarian. Who could resist a quick browse?

Livre* versus *bouquin. The term *bouquin*, derived from the Dutch *boekijn* (small book), now generally refers to a volume of little value or a secondhand book, hence the difference between a *bouquinerie*, selling used books, and a *librairie*, selling brand-new ones.

A long tradition. Paris's *bouquinistes* are descendants of the street vendors of the French *Ancien Régime* (Old Order). They often encountered opposition from bookstore associations and central government keen to crack down on any parallel markets that might escape censorship, and were only officially established in 1859.

Dark green. The green color of the *bouquinistes*' display boxes is typical for Parisian street furniture that uses the same color scheme, such as metro station signs, Wallace public drinking fountains, and Morris advertising columns once used to display theater posters.

Fun fact. The *bouquinistes*' symbol is a lizard looking at a sword. The lizard represents the *bouquinistes* themselves, constantly seeking the sun to sell their books, while the sword stands for their aspiration to the noble vocation of bookseller, a profession that at the time had been granted the privilege of bearing one.

Bibliothèque François Mitterrand

The futuristic Bibliothèque François Mitterrand, including the nouvelle BnF (new National Library of France), was opened in the 13th *arrondissement* by the then President of the Republic in 1995. It has become the hub around which Paris Rive Gauche, the capital's most modern neighborhood, has continued to develop.

The project. Designed in a minimalist style by the French architect Dominique Perrault, it consists of four skyscrapers, each 260 ft (79 m) tall and shaped like open books, named the towers of Times, Laws, Numbers, and Letters, respectively. **A 2½-acre (1-hectare) garden** has been laid out in the middle and is open to the public.

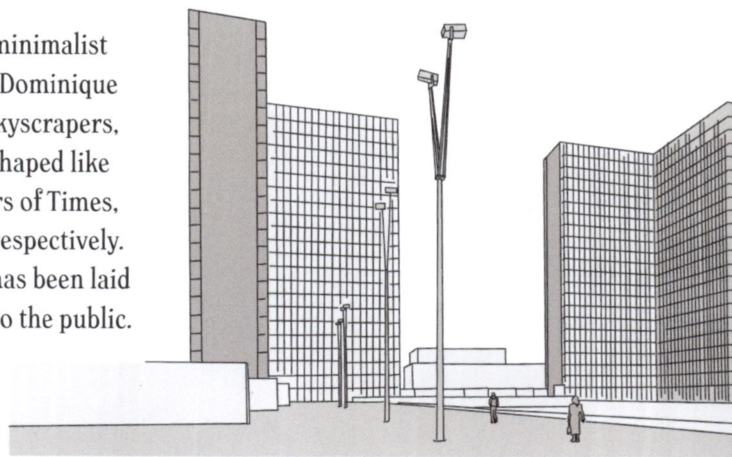

Other tall buildings in the area. Make sure not to miss the Tour M6B2, which changes colors depending on the angle of the sun; the impressive Tours Duo (Ateliers Jean Nouvel); Le Nid (The Nest), an original structure covered in branch-like structures; and the bridge-building in which the editorial office of the *Le Monde* daily newspaper is now based.

Startup nation. Tucked away inside some old railroad buildings from the 1920s located near the library, you will find Station F, the world's biggest startup campus, founded by the billionaire French entrepreneur Xavier Niel, the head of the Free telecommunications company in France.

Les Grands Moulins. These old industrial mill buildings dating back to the First World War (and an adjacent flour warehouse) now house lecture theaters, a library, and administrative offices for Paris Diderot University, in a part of the neighborhood that is extremely popular with students.

Other beautiful libraries

BnF Richelieu. The historic original site of the Bibliothèque nationale de France (rue Vivienne) reopened to the public after a twelve-year renovation. Everyone should visit the Salle Ovale (Oval Room, but appropriately nicknamed Oval Paradise) at least once in their life.

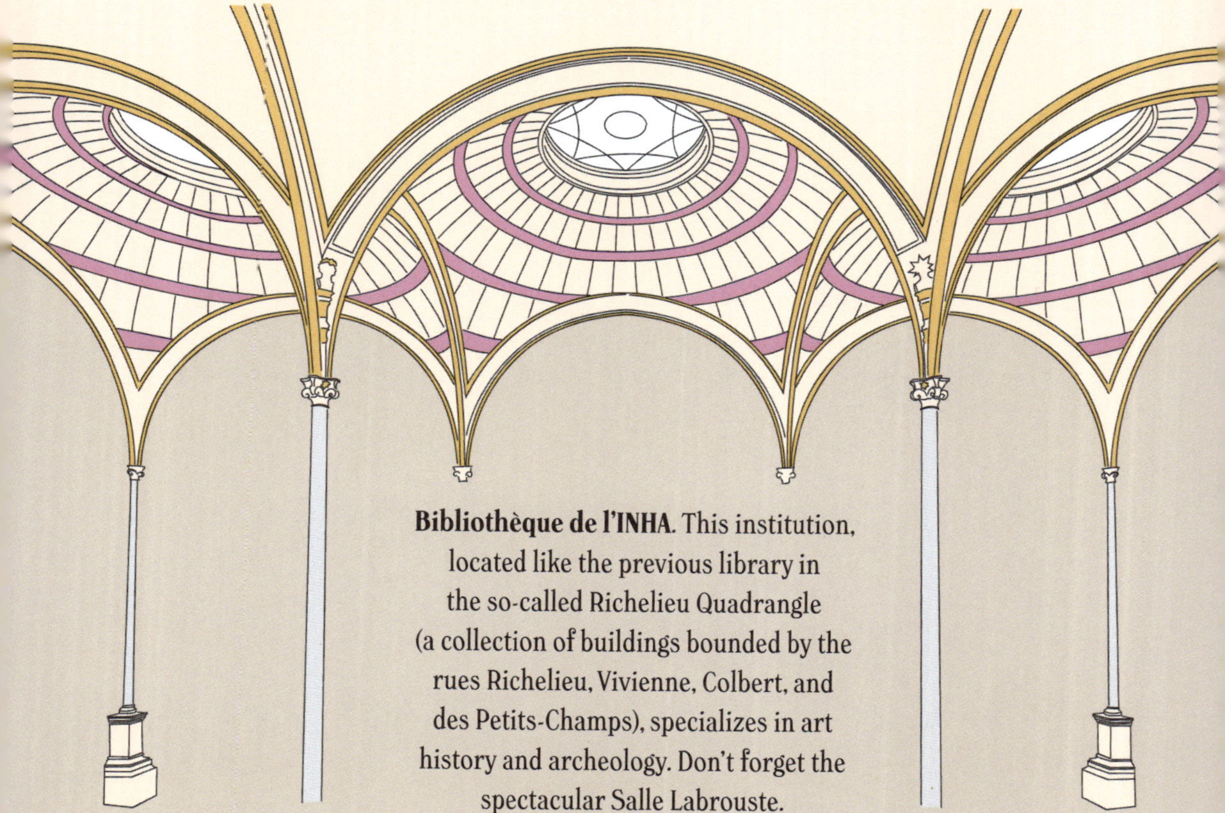

Bibliothèque de l'INHA. This institution, located like the previous library in the so-called Richelieu Quadrangle (a collection of buildings bounded by the rues Richelieu, Vivienne, Colbert, and des Petits-Champs), specializes in art history and archeology. Don't forget the spectacular Salle Labrouste.

Bibliothèque Sainte-Geneviève. This collection focused on literature and the humanities is not far from the Panthéon in a splendid building over 500 years old that is now listed as a historic monument.

Bibliothèque Mazarine. The doors to France's oldest public library have been open to readers since 1643 on an enviable site beside the picturesque Quai de Conti. With its 40,000 volumes, it was at one time the largest in Europe.

***Médiathèques* (multimedia libraries).** These local cultural centers, which lend books, movies, and music to the public, are an essential part of French daily life. One of the most famous is the Médiathèque Françoise Sagan, which was built on the site of the former leper colony of Saint-Lazare prison in the 10th *arrondissement.*

Shakespeare and Company. Not a library, but this amazing bookstore with its wooden shelves laden with books just a stone's throw from Notre-Dame has become a historic monument in Paris and an obligatory stop for any self-respecting book lover and tourist.

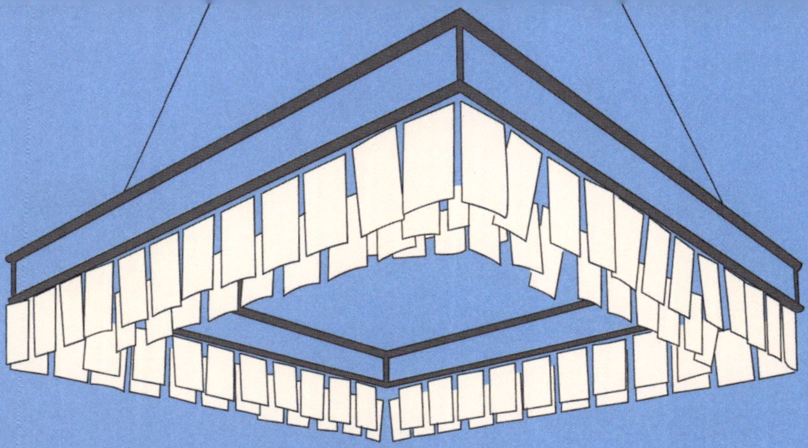

Book events in Paris

Festival du Livre de Paris (Paris Book Festival). The French equivalent of Germany's Frankfurt Book Fair is the biggest national event devoted to books and reading. It is currently held in the Grand Palais Éphémère, a temporary exhibition hall erected at the far end of the Champ de Mars.

Marché de la Poésie (Poetry Festival). This annual event dedicated to poetry is held on Place Saint-Sulpice. It is simpler and more intimate than other cultural events, and the most authentic and alternative, thanks in part to the judicious amounts of alcohol in circulation among publishers' booths.

Salon du Livre Jeunesse (Children's Book Fair). This fair is held in the decidedly arty suburb of Montreuil. It is an enormous success every year and testament to the quality and passion of France's editors and authors of illustrated books.

Paris Manga. This enormous trade fair dedicated to pop culture (from Japanese *manga* to science fiction) has become a classic for fans of the genre. It is currently held at Paris Nord Villepinte, the biggest exhibition center in France.

Maison de la Poésie (House of Poetry). Located within the Théâtre Molière on the charming Passage Molière, this place dedicated to creating, disseminating, and experiencing literature is undoubtedly one of the liveliest and most stimulating cultural centers in the capital.

Vintage books. If you're a fan of antiquarian tomes, or just looking for secondhand books at unbeatable prices, the perfect market awaits on the charming Parc Georges Brassens in the 15th *arrondissement*, held every Sunday.

Versailles

The unmissable Palace of Versailles, the main residence of Kings Louis XIV, XV, and XVI and a symbol of the French *Ancien Régime* (Old Order), is only 10 miles (16 km) southwest of Paris.

It is one of the finest examples of modern classical architecture in the world and famous for its lavish decor and immense gardens laid out in the French style.

Hall of Mirrors. The gigantic hall of the Galerie des Glaces is decorated with 357 mirrors and windows and is one of the most impressive rooms in the palace, not merely for its size and the extravagance of its decor, but also for its picturesque views of the gardens and the Grand Canal.

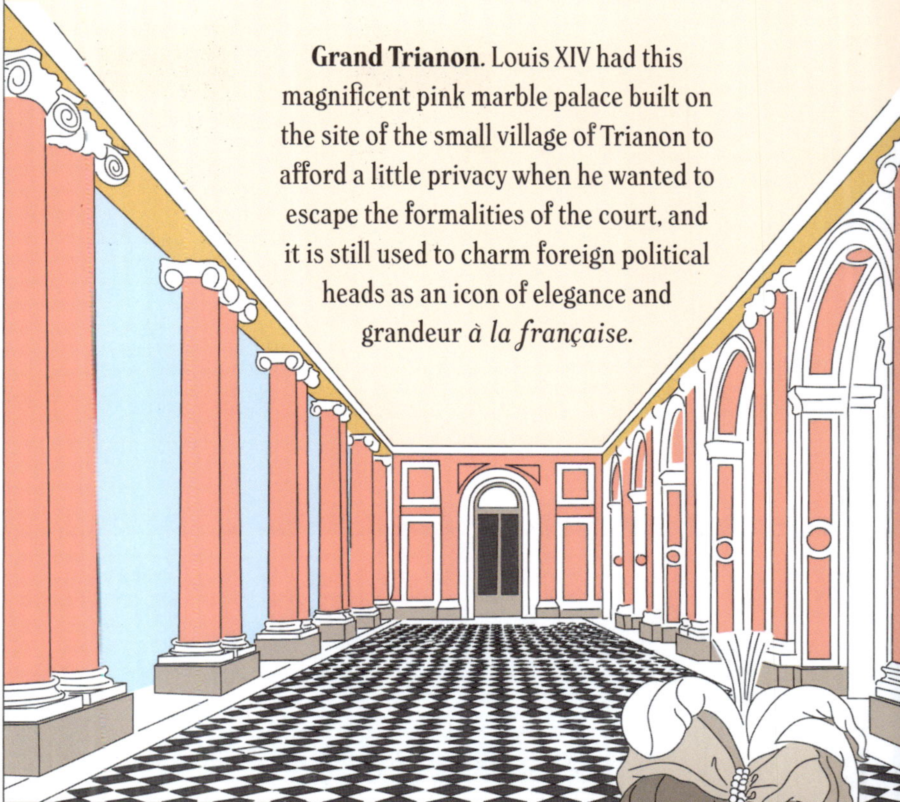

Grand Trianon. Louis XIV had this magnificent pink marble palace built on the site of the small village of Trianon to afford a little privacy when he wanted to escape the formalities of the court, and it is still used to charm foreign political heads as an icon of elegance and grandeur *à la française.*

Marie Antoinette. The "Austrian" queen, a lover of country living skillfully conjured up in pop-culture style in Sofia Coppola's movie of 2006, had a residence built just over a mile (2 km) from the Palace of Versailles, designed by her own hand as an exact replica of a Norman village, complete with small cottages and an artificial lake.

Not just a palace. The town of Versailles is not without its charms. Noted for its great elegance (and even perhaps a little snobbishness), it has been home for some three centuries to the lovely Notre-Dame market, among a host of bustling cafés, cobbled streets, and charming antiques stores.

Giverny

Giverny is an easy train journey of just over an hour from Paris's Gare Saint-Lazare station. This small Norman village, with its unique light, became justly famous as the place to which Impressionist painter Claude Monet was drawn and where he made his home from 1883 until his death in 1926.

Claude Monet's house. Admire the vibrancy of the famous "blue salon" (Petit Salon Bleu), the yellow furniture in the dining room, and the artist's studio, but you won't want to miss the Japanese-style gardens and the small, panoramic bridge looking out over the waterlilies that inspired his most famous paintings.

Hôtel Baudy. A host of artists (including Cézanne and Rodin) followed in Monet's footsteps and visited Giverny to seek inspiration. Most stayed in this hotel (which is now a bar and restaurant) and enjoyed the splendid variety of roses in its romantic gardens.

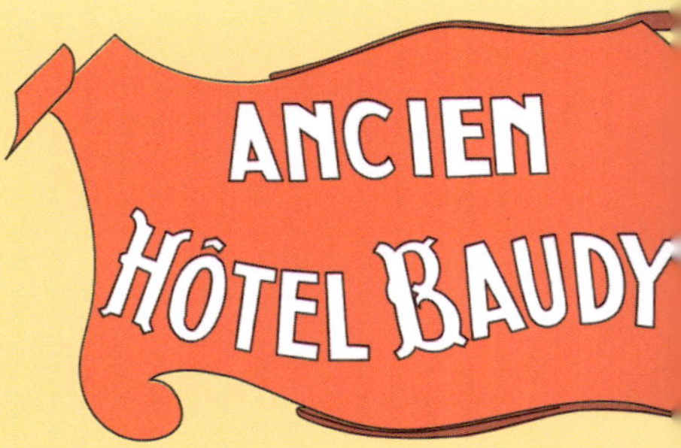

Le Vieux Moulin. The old water mill in Vernon, a village a couple of miles outside Giverny, is a spectacular, half-timbered house balanced across two piers of what was once a bridge over the Seine. It was painted by Claude Monet from his studio-boat in 1883, the year he moved to Normandy.

Auvers-sur-Oise. This picturesque village is also about an hour away by train from Paris (from the Gare du Nord this time), and it was here that Vincent van Gogh lived, died, and was buried. The Dutch artist painted *Wheatfield with Crows*, his last great canvas here, and it is possible that the fatal shot was fired in this very field.

Champagne

One of the world's most famous wine regions is located just a few dozen miles northeast of Paris. The most famous Champagne houses are scattered among the rolling hills, picturesque villages, and charming towns of the area, keeping guard over miles of underground wine-filled cellars that are truly a world heritage site.

Caves de Champagne. Mumm, Moët & Chandon, and Ruinart are just some of the famous Champagne houses that cosset their precious bottles, sheltered from light and heat, in the cellars of Reims (with 75 miles/120 km of subterranean galleries dug out of the chalk) and Épernay, the capital of Champagne—a sight not to be missed.

Notre-Dame de Reims. For eight centuries, the kings of France were crowned in one of the most majestic and spectacular examples of French Gothic architecture. On the west facade, you will find the *Ange au Sourire* (smiling angel), a statue made famous by photographs that showed it before and after the bomb damage it suffered during the First World War.

Dom Pérignon. In Hautvillers, on the southern slopes of the Montagne de Reims, you will find a Benedictine abbey, once home to the monk who devised a technique for blending grapes to improve wines, along with a way of reinforcing wine bottles to prevent them exploding (although some believe sparkling wine was invented by British physician Christopher Merret). Today it is the most famous Champagne house in the world.

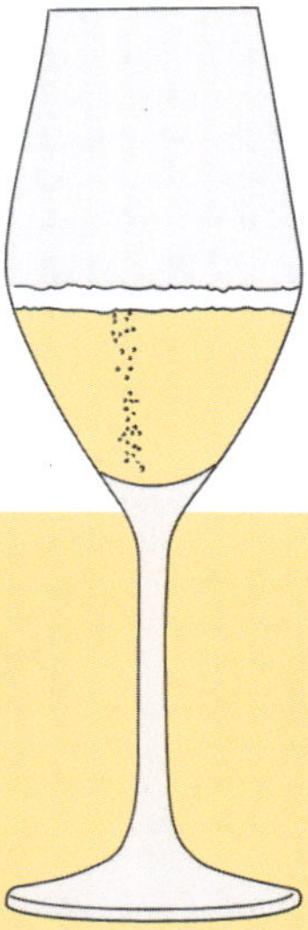

Coupe or flûte? Should you go for the famous champagne *coupe*, which does not preserve either bubbles or aromas well, or opt for the *flûte*, which has few fans among wine-tasters due to its limited practical use? The perfect glass falls between these two options—what you'll find in use in most local bars and restaurants is the tulip glass.

Lac du Der-Chantecoq. This beautiful artificial lake (the largest in Europe, and far bigger than the more famous one at Annecy) is unfairly neglected by tourists, although it has become a very popular spot with ornithologists. More than anything, though, it is the beach of choice for locals when the weather is clement.

At the seaside in Deauville

Thanks to attractions that include the Palais des Congrès convention center, along with its famous casino, splendid hotels, villas, marinas, golf courses, racecourse, and nightclubs, this small seaside resort on the English Channel has gained a reputation as one of the most stylish in France and is known as "Paris by the beach."

Etablissement des Bains de Mer. The high temple of beach life in Deauville, with its colonnades, mosaic-encrusted pools, and Art Deco bathing huts was built in 1923. Its famous wooden boardwalk overlooking the sea becomes a catwalk for stars of the American Film Festival.

Villa Strassburger. This spectacular villa was built by Baron Henri de Rothschild in 1907. It is considered the forerunner of the manor houses that became typical of the region and its elaborate lines, checkered brick and stone first floor, and half-timbered upper stories continue to charm visitors.

Les Franciscaines. This modern cultural center opened its doors inside a former convent in 2021. It includes a museum, restaurant, reading room enclosed within a magnificent cloister, and media center specializing in equestrian sports, cinema, entertainment, photography, and children's literature.

Cabourg. The famous French author Marcel Proust spent his "therapeutic" vacations by the sea, staying in room 414 of the luxurious Grand Hôtel in this small seaside town, which was to serve as inspiration for Balbec in his novel *A la recherche du temps perdu* (*In Search of Lost Time*). Located just a few miles south of Deauville, it is a must-see, a place of timeless charm.

Honfleur. This city just a few miles north of Deauville is an absolute gem and was very popular with painters, including the Impressionists. Don't miss the Vieux-Bassin (old port) with its picturesque lanes and typical small restaurants.

Brasseries and bistros

BRASSERIE
de Paris

Paris would not be Paris without the bars, brasseries, bistros, and restaurants that for many locals are a natural extension of their apartments, which are often too small to facilitate a proper social life. Many people remain unsure of the difference between these types of establishment and risk not knowing what to expect.

Vins
Plats du Jour

The brasserie. Historically, brasseries were places where beer was brewed on site (*brasserie* meaning "brewhouse," although they are more than that). Unlike other establishments, they now serve a wide selection of hot and cold food from morning until late evening, with continuous service.

Boeuf Bourguignon

Three typical dishes to order in a brasserie:

1) *Choucroute garnie*: Pork prepared in various different ways, accompanied by sauerkraut.
2) *Bœuf bourguignon*: Beef stewed in red wine.
3) *Blanquette de veau*: Veal simmered and served in a *velouté* sauce made with butter and flour.

The bistro. This kind of restaurant, whose name is derived from Russian Быстро (bystro – quickly), a phrase used by Napoleonic-era Russian hussars who thought French service too slow, was the forerunner of today's fast-food joints. The menu is shorter and less elaborate than in a brasserie, and the kitchen is only open at mealtimes.

Croque Madame

Quiche Lorraine

Three typical bistro dishes to order:
1) *Croque-monsieur*: A grilled sandwich of ham, cheese, and *béchamel* sauce (there is also a version with egg, known as a *croque-madame*).
2) *Quiche lorraine*: The classic savory tart, made with eggs, sour cream, and pork belly bacon.
3) *Omelette*: Usually plain, but also made with ham and cheese.

Meet the Parisians: The waiter

Parisian waiters have a mixed reputation with tourists, who are sometimes astonished at how customers can be treated so sneeringly, and indeed with Parisians themselves, who would much rather live in New York, as long as they are not expected to leave a tip.

"Do you speak *touriste*?" Amid concerns about negative publicity from tourists, the city authorities published a guide in 2013 (the latest edition is from 2022) that sought to encourage hospitality workers to be more polite to their customers and try to manage a few words of English ...

A hellish job. In response to criticism from readers, the British daily newspaper *The Guardian* published an article defending Parisian waitstaff, many of whom were reported to be braving 10-mile (17-km) commutes and 15-hour shifts to serve 200 customers every day, all for €1,200 ($1,440) a month.

Three things that might happen to you in a Parisian restaurant. 1) You are ignored. You take a seat and everyone else gets served but you, and only you, are not. 2) You are just about to finish eating, chatting comfortably while waiting to take your last bite, and your plate is snatched away from under your nose. 3) The waiter recites the day's specials from memory at lightning speed (it is the two-hundredth time that day they have done it) and when you ask them to repeat it, they emit a long, sarcastic sigh to your face.

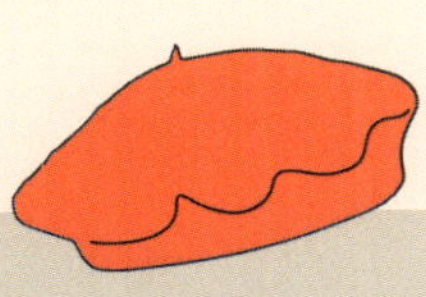

"Here, the customer's *never* right." In one of the first scenes in the popular TV series *Emily in Paris*, our heroine finds herself in a brasserie and asks the waiter to cook her steak a little more (she wants it medium, not rare), but her request is refused. Sorry, Emily, but you're in Paris, not America!

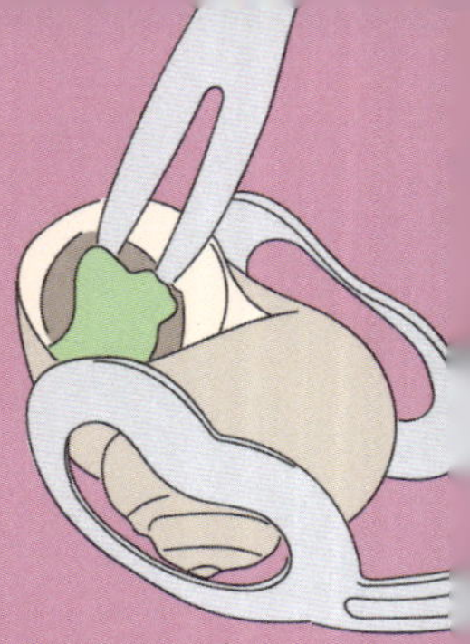

Escargots

Snails are an icon of French cuisine and a source of intense curiosity to the non-French diner. This timeless classic often appears on the menus of Parisian brasseries, even though it is essentially a local dish which is prepared according to the region.

Cassolette d'escargots

Three (of the many) ways to cook *escargots*.
1) *À la bourguignonne*, the great classic: The snails are placed back in their shells, doused in butter, garlic, and parsley, and then baked in the oven.
2) *Feuilleté d'escargots*: The snails are baked without shells in little round puff pastry cases.
3) *Cassolette d'escargots*: A *cassolette* is a small china dish used in dozens of recipes, and snail dishes are no exception. White or red wine, Brie cheese, or even *foie gras* may be involved.

à la Bourguignonne

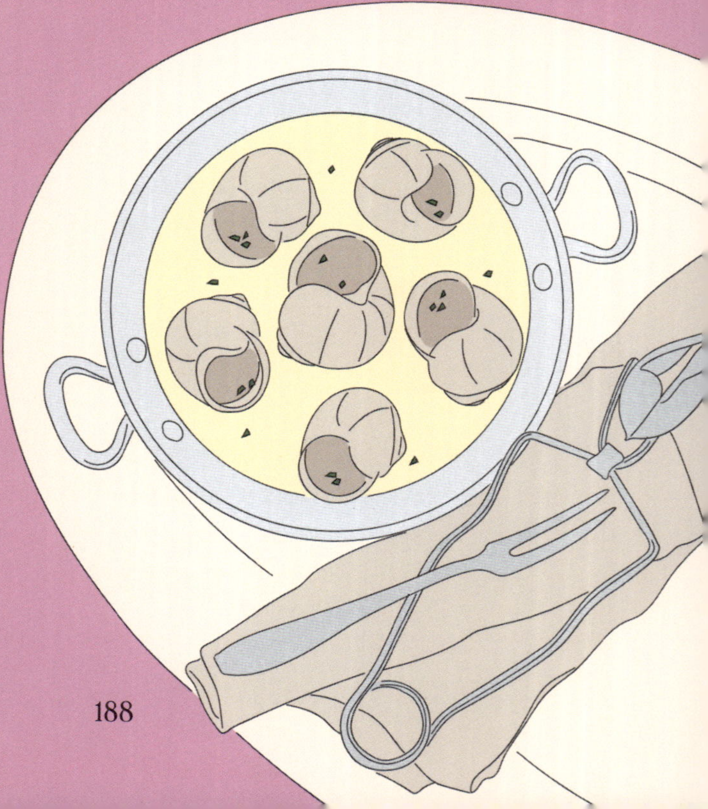

Feuilleté d'escargots

Natural viagra. Aphrodisiac properties have been attributed to snails from ancient Roman times until the **nineteenth century, so much** so that they were considered powerful sexual stimulants despite being almost always eaten with prodigious amounts of garlic.

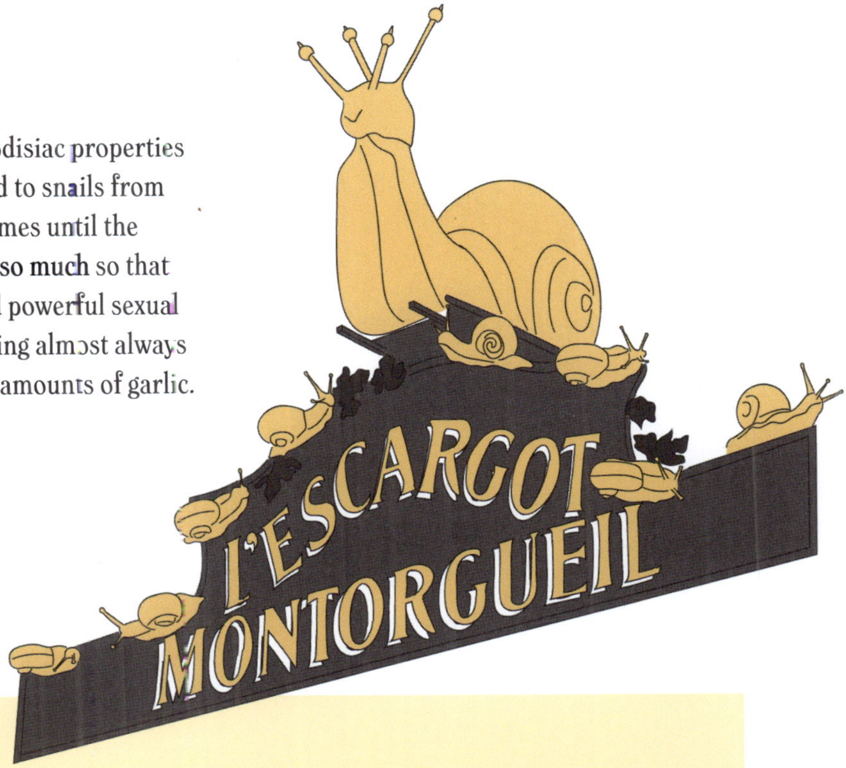

L'Escargot Montorgueil. This historic Parisian restaurant specializing in shellfish (which is impossible to miss, given the enormous snail keeping watch over the entrance) cast its spell over many of the great names of the 1900s, including Sarah Bernhardt, Marcel Proust, French actor Sacha Guitry, and Salvador Dalí, all of whom were loyal patrons.

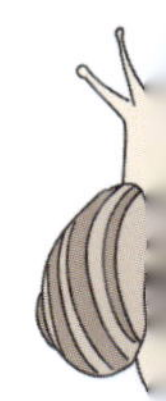

Sweet snails? Those with a sweet tooth know that *viennnoiserie* (Danish pastries) are in good company with the *croissant* and *pain au chocolat* as classic French baked goods. These snail-shaped confections are made of leavened flaky pastry to which custard and raisins (*pain aux raisins*) or chocolate chips are added.

Pain aux raisins

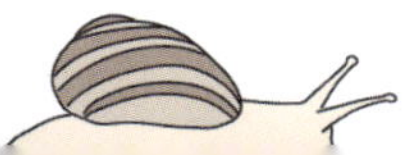

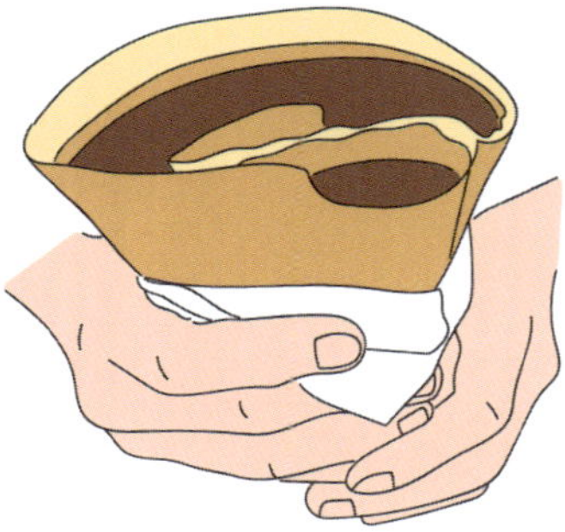

Crêpes

Whether eaten hot or cold, savory or plain, as a main course, dessert, or, especially in Paris, street food, the *crêpe* is yet another icon of French cuisine and the finest regional delicacy to come out of Brittany.

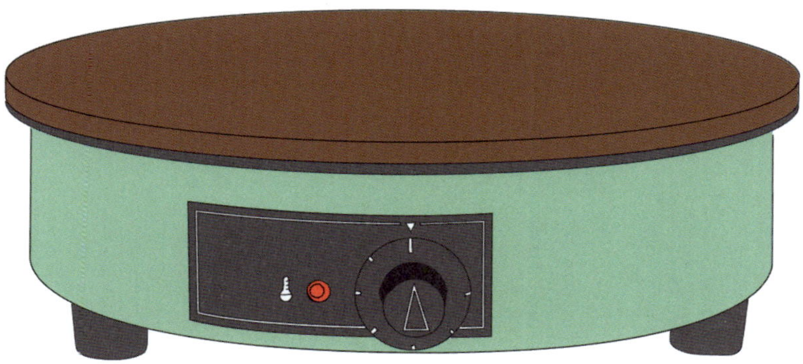

Three (typically Breton) tools for making crêpes. 1) The Billig crêpe maker (or *crêpière*) is the circular cast-iron plate on which the crêpe batter is spread. 2) The *rozell* is the T-shaped wooden spreader used to coat the *crêpière* with batter (ideally with a single turn of the wrist). 3) The *spanell* is the (wooden or metal) spatula used to flip and fold the *crêpe*.

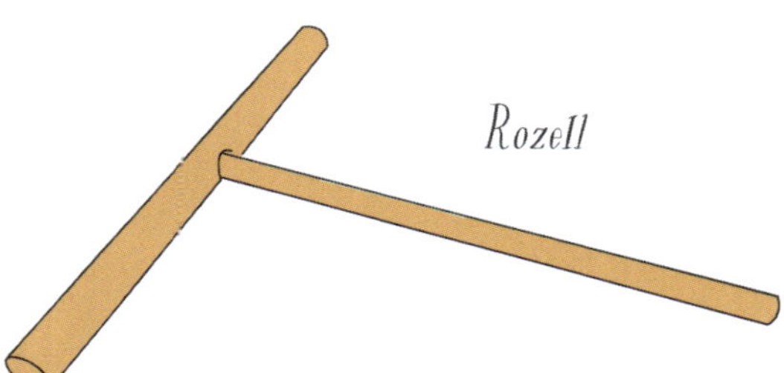

***Crêpe* or *galette*?** Do not mix them up! A *crêpe* is made with wheat flour and is generally sweet (although a few exceptions apply), whereas a *galette*, as typically eaten in Brittany, is made with buckwheat flour and is always eaten as a savory treat.

Bolée de cidre. Cider, an alcoholic drink made by fermenting apple juice, may be sweet or dry and is a typical accompaniment to *galettes*. Visit a Breton *crêperie* and you will generally find it served in unusual stoneware bowls.

Crêpes Suzette. This is one of the most famous French desserts in the world. A *crêpe* is accompanied by a sauce made from caramelized sugar, butter, the juice and zest of an orange, and Grand Marnier liqueur, usually served flambéed.

Crêpe Suzette

La Chandeleur. Candlemas (or the Feast of the Presentation of Jesus Christ) is celebrated on February 2, forty days after Christmas, as one of the occasions in the year when the French come together to eat *crêpes*. They are also mandatory at Mardi Gras.

French cheese

What would France be without its impressive (may one say even a little excessive?) list of at least 1,200 different kinds of cheese? Decent bread and a good cheese are the embodiment of homesickness for the French when they're not at home (like al dente pasta for Italians, a cup of tea for the British, and a decent burger for Americans).

Vieux Boulogne

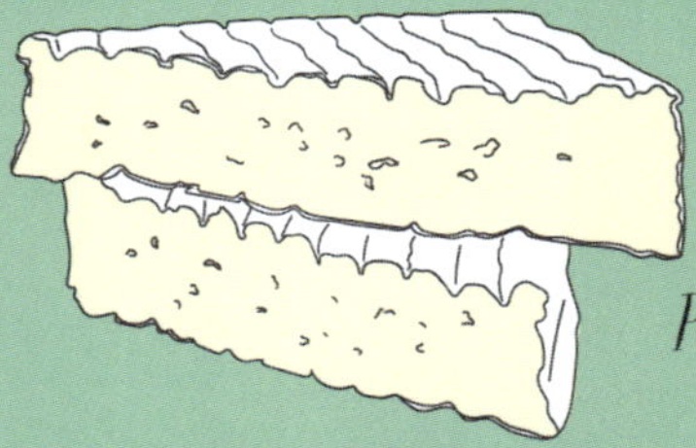

Pont l'Evêque AOP

The world's top five smelliest cheeses are all French, so be warned. 1) *Vieux Boulogne*: with 7–9 weeks of aging; 2) *Pont l'Evêque AOP*: 6 weeks of aging; 3) *Camembert de Normandie AOP*: 21 days of aging; 4) *Munster*: 3 weeks of aging; 5) *Brie de Meaux AOP*: 4–8 weeks of aging.

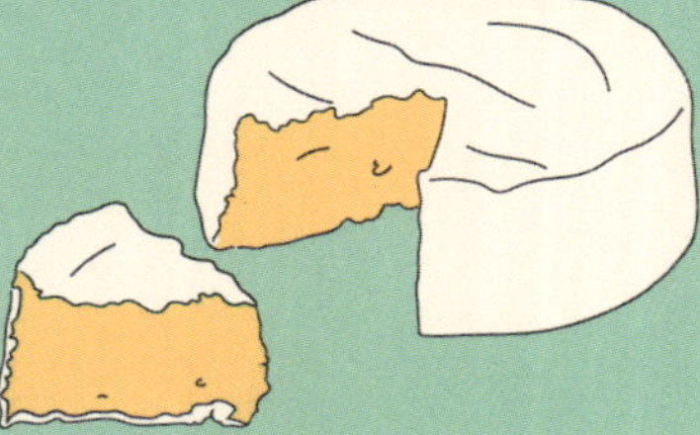

Camembert de Normandie AOP

Munster

Brie de Meaux AOP

Every cheese is improved by a good glass of wine, and in France you're spoilt for choice, of course, from the "less sunny" reds of the Loire Valley to a classic Bordeaux, from the whites of Alsace to the (slightly overpriced) wines of Burgundy, from the Côtes du Rhône to the Côtes de Provence.

Three cheese-based French dishes:

1) *Tartiflette* is a Savoyard recipe made with potatoes, onion, and pancetta, all of which are then baked *au gratin* with Reblochon cheese.

2) *Raclette* is a cheese of Swiss origin that is melted under a special grill, poured over boiled potatoes, and then eaten with dried meats.

3) *Mont d'Or au four* is a soft cheese made from cow's milk that is baked in the oven with a little white wine and eaten with bread.

The scourge of *Emmental rapé*. The French use grated Emmental like the Italians use Parmesan (i.e., absolutely everywhere): on pasta, on toast, on hot dogs, in gratins, and to the utter horror of Italians even in *soupe de poisson* (fish soup). *De gustibus ...*

Exotic food

Paris is a multicultural metropolis and its cultural diversity is reflected in the food on offer. In addition to the many Asian restaurants (a long-established presence), exotic food is becoming both increasingly fashionable in the capital and expensive as a result.

Hamburger mania. McDonald's claim that France is the brand's second-largest market in the world after the United States, and you'll find so-called "gourmet burger" places everywhere now. This is less of a surprise if you consider that a hamburger = bread+meat+cheese. Where else would you eat that, if not in France?

Hamburger gourmet

Couscous. A firm French favorite, especially with students thanks to its affordable price and generous portions. As a result of widespread immigration from Northwest Africa to the capital, there is no shortage of places to eat couscous, and some bars even dish it out for free during happy hour.

Couscous

Latin America in Paris. South American dishes are slowly gaining a foothold in the capital. After the seemingly endless fashion for Mexican restaurants, fast food and street food are now coming into their own, as is certainly the case with tacos, for example, or the increasingly popular Argentinian empanadas.

Poke bowls and healthy food. Healthy eating is a big trend in Paris, from vegan restaurants serving seasonal fruit and vegetables to an enthusiasm for matcha, vitamins, and superfoods, and the current obsession for poke bowls, a Hawaiian dish made with marinated raw fish, rice, and exotic vegetables.

Poulet braisé. Portuguese may have less of a presence than other ethnic cuisines, but it is still very popular in Paris. Of all the dishes, each more delicious than the last, marinated roast chicken remains an enduring classic. A must-try!

Italy in Paris

Reports suggest that the French are among the biggest consumers of pizza in the world, eating even more than the Italians. Not only are more and more Neapolitan pizzerias and Italian restaurants (run by Italians) popping up in Paris, there are also more delis selling typical Italian products; it must be love.

The Big Mamma empire. Paris's largest Italian restaurant chain was founded by Victor Lugger and Tigrane Seydoux. Since 2015, they've opened a dozen packed venues, including La Felicità, a 50,000-square-ft (4,500-square-m) dining hall with seven restaurants serving 1,500–3,000 daily covers.

Burratà. Yes, you read that right, with an accent on the "a." These days, it is more of an obsession than a passion for a lot of Parisians, who are quite happy to pay €6, €7, or even €8 for a single piece. They put it on pizza, in salads, you name it, and even go to special mozzarella bars to sample it. They might have 1,200 kinds of cheese, but they don't have *burratà*.

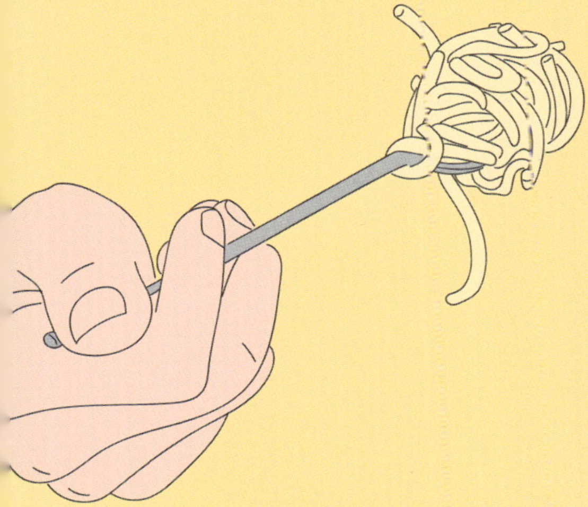

Less is more. The French have traditionally considered Italian cuisine "simple" (indeed, even *basique*, which is not necessarily a compliment), but it is now finding a place in the hearts of the great chefs from the north side of the Alps, including the likes of the legendary Alain Ducasse, for example, who elected to open Italian restaurant Cucina (sadly, now closed) in the heart of the Latin Quarter.

CUCINA

Carbonarà. Even though some French websites suggest that cream was not eliminated from the recipe until the 1980s, the days of *crème fraîche* in *carbo* are thankfully at an end. The original is now ubiquitous in Paris (try it at Ida or Racines), but the coast is not completely clear, as there's always the risk of encountering a dubious veggie version.

Eataly. Oscar Farinetti's brand hit Paris in 2019 (not that there was much need for it, given what was already on offer) with over 40,000 square feet (4,000 square meters) of dining area over three floors in the heart of Le Marais, complete with a cookery school and (how did we survive without it?) a mozzarella-making workshop.

Food markets

Shopping at the market is an intrinsic part of French, and indeed Parisian, daily life. You're spoilt for choice, with markets open all day, every day, outdoors and indoors, along with Marché des Enfants Rouges (see page 67), which is the oldest, and Marché d'Aligre (see page 118). Here are a few others to check out.

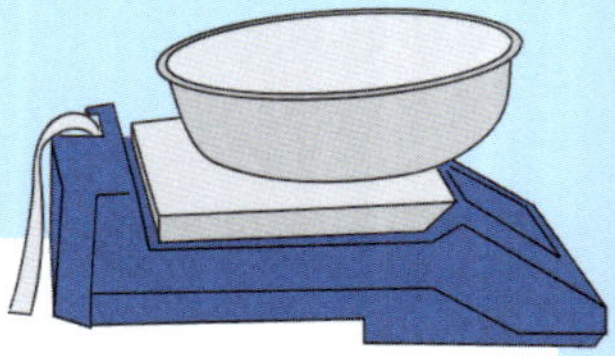

The cheapest. Stroll among the stalls beneath the metro overpass at Barbès-Rochechouart station and you will hear the cry "One Euro the kilo!" This is not the place for you if you don't like crowds, however, as it is one of the busiest markets in Paris.

The most organic. The beautiful Marché des Batignolles is *bobo* central and a haven for lovers of organic and zero-food-miles fruit and veg, but might not suit every pocket.

The biggest. The Marché Saint-Quentin is the largest covered market in Paris, with the advantage of having practically everything all under one roof, including exotic hot food stalls from Africa to Italy, from couscous to falafel.

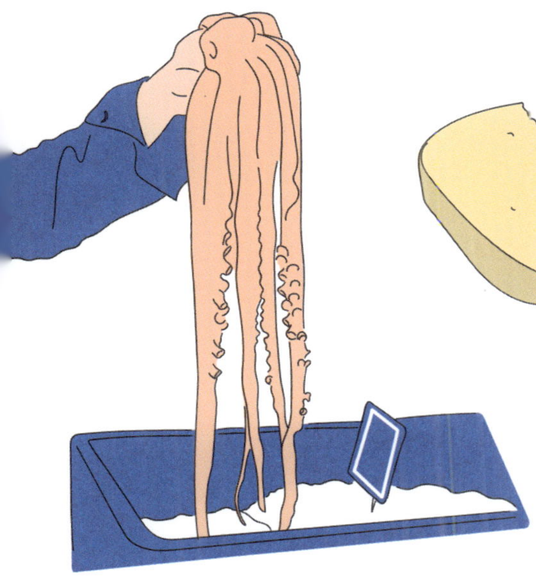

The most elegant. The renovated Halle Secrétan and the historic Marché Saint-Germain are two next-generation covered markets in which traditional food stalls rub shoulders with upmarket boutiques more reminiscent of shopping malls.

Le Douze. Inspired by New York's food courts, this modern temple to French produce has taken up residence in the old Reuilly-Diderot military barracks. You really do get dinner and a show.

Fête de la Musique

For Parisians, this is one of the most anticipated and popular events of the year. In celebration of the beginning of summer, every June 21 people of all ages throng the streets, and the city, including some unusual spots that would normally be entirely inaccessible, is transformed into a string of stages featuring both professional and amateur musicians.

Music everywhere: "Music will be everywhere, concerts nowhere" was the watchword of French composer Maurice Fleuret, a colleague of Jack Lang, the famous socialist Minister of Culture of the time, when the first music festival was organized in 1982.

International success. To mark the European Year of Music in 1985, the foundations were laid to make the Fête de la Musique a European event; the statute was signed in Budapest in 1997, opening the event to all who wished to take part. Fewer than ten years later, the format had been adopted by eighty-five countries worldwide.

Solidays. This musical event, "three days of music and solidarity," held at the Longchamp racecourse, was first organized in 1999 by an association involved in preventing and fighting AIDS, and it has become popular with Parisians, especially young people.

Rock en Seine. This rock music festival, which attracts 40,000 spectators per day to the magnificent grounds laid out by André Le Nôtre at Parc de Saint-Cloud, has been a summer institution in Paris since 2003. It was here that the Gallagher brothers had the enormous bust-up that brought legendary 1990s band Oasis to an end.

ROCK en SEINE

DON'T MISS

Fête des Vendanges de Montmartre

Every second weekend in October since 1934, the local council of the 18th *arrondissement* has organized the Montmartre Harvest Festival, a large and well-attended event in the local streets to celebrate the arrival of the *cuvées* brought down from Clos-Montmartre, the small but historic vineyard located on the eponymous Parisian hill.

Vendanges

The Montmartre vineyard. Located on the northern slopes of the hill on which the Sacré-Cœur proudly stands, there is a vineyard. It is now just a small plot of land of about ½ acre (approx. 2,000 square meters), but the local council has managed with some difficulty to save it from being paved over.

If you are keen to take part, remember the local saying "*C'est du vin de Montmartre/Qui en boit pinte en pisse quart*" (It's wine from Montmartre, drink a pint, pee a quart)—as good a way as any of paying homage to its diuretic properties, presumably?

C'est de la piquette. This is the slang term for poor-quality table wine, with *piquette* historically referring to a light-bodied wine once made by adding water to grape pomace, although it is also the name given to a young and slightly sparkling wine made with grapes from the hills of Belleville.

Beaujolais nouveau. Talking of wine of less than noble heritage, if you happen to find yourself in Paris on the third Thursday in November, you'll be swimming in it! This young red wine of debatable flavor is produced in the eponymous region near Lyon.

It's not just about wine. Since the 2000s, the Montmartre Harvest Festival has had a different theme each year (love, peace, liberty, the planet, equality) for which the organizers offer relevant activities, workshops, and shows.

La Nuit Blanche

The traditional white night, or all-nighter, a Parisian event not to be missed, was traditionally always held on the night between the Saturday and Sunday of the first weekend in October until 2023, when it moved to the first weekend in June. The motive was pretty obvious: they were hoping for some decent weather!

Over twenty years! Nuit Blanche, launched in 2002 under mayor Bertrand Delanoë, has involved more than 4,000 artists, staging at least 2,000 annual events—from installations to performances—transforming the city into a vast open-air festival.

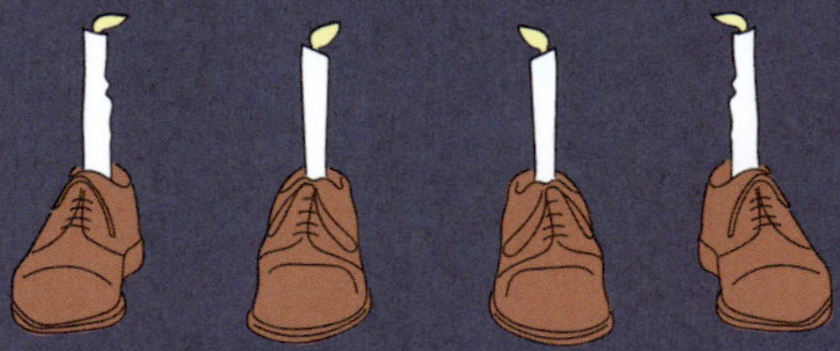

La Nuit des Musées. More than 200 Parisian museums and monuments open their doors to the public for free on one Saturday evening a year as part of European Museum Night, and if you miss the date, don't panic as there is free admission to almost all museums in Paris on the first Sunday of every month!

Three other arty events not to be missed:
1) Paris Fashion Week, the last of the "big four" (the most prestigious fashion meets in the world); 2) Paris Design Week, a week devoted to new trends in contemporary design; 3) Paris Photo, an international festival celebrating classic and contemporary photography.

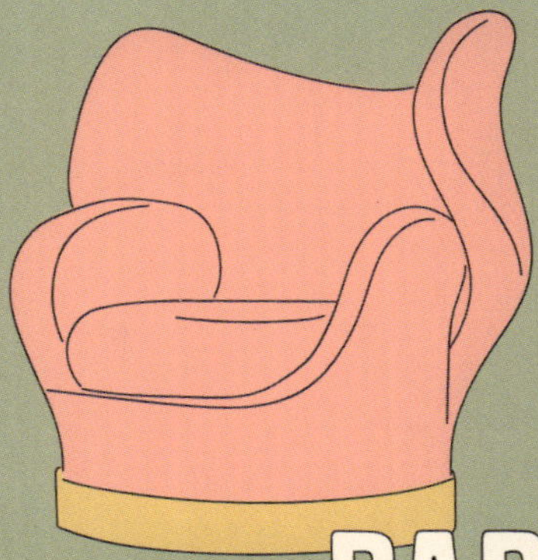

PARIS DESIGN WEEK

Paris leads the way. The first Nuit Blanche, held in 2002, had been suggested to Mayor Delanoë by Christophe Girard, his cultural deputy and, from the following year, the format was replicated in Rome, Brussels, Leeds, Malaga, and a host of other cities around the world.

DON'T MISS

Paris-Plages

A classic since 2002. Every summer, when most of the residents, along with their cars, flee Paris, the city undergoes a sea change and transforms into a holiday resort for a couple of months. The banks of the Seine and the city's watercourses are strewn with sand, parasols, and deck chairs, and the end results can be unsettling.

Parc Rives de Seine. From the Pont des Arts to the Pont de Sully (Right Bank) and from Solférino to the Pont Alexandre III (Left Bank), the Seine is turned into an esplanade worthy of any (French) seaside resort. Pick your way between picnic tables, palm trees, and parasols as you enjoy exclusive views of gems like Notre-Dame, the Louvre, and the Musée d'Orsay.

Bassin de la Villette. The Paris-Plages infrastructure is not restricted to the banks of the Seine, and can be found as far afield as the 19th *arrondissement.* Three enormous pools of different depths await on the Quai de Loire (on the Canal de l'Ourcq), for example, a perfect way to cool off during a typical Parisian summer heatwave ...

Where Saint-Quentin leads … Just for once, Paris wasn't the first to come up with the idea. The seed for Operation Paris-Plages was sown in this city in northern France, where a beach was created on the Place de l'Hôtel-de-Ville in 1996 to help counter the economic difficulties facing some of its residents.

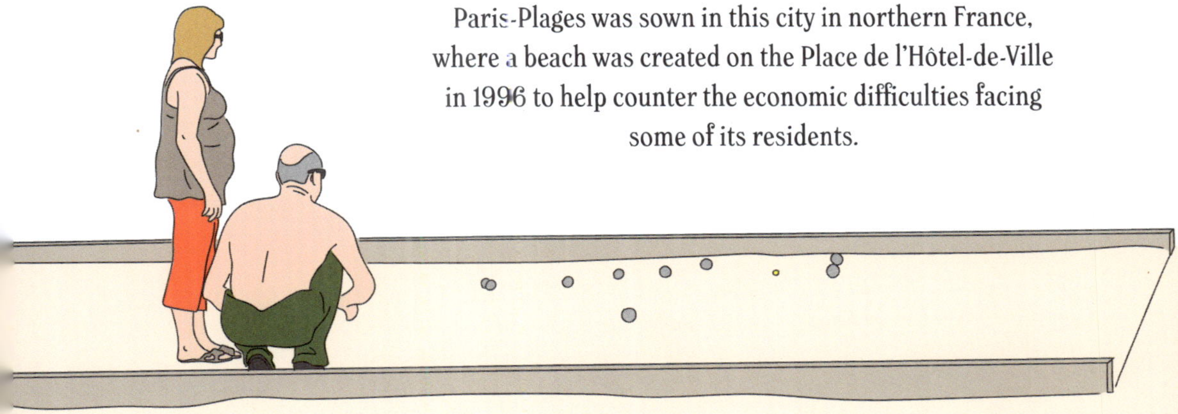

Brazil at the Hôtel de Ville. These four beach volleyball courts right in front of the entrance to Paris's City Hall, a stone's throw from Notre-Dame and the Conciergerie, have been an icon of Paris-Plages for some years. It is considered by some as an original curiosity, by others as an eyesore.

Paris Plages

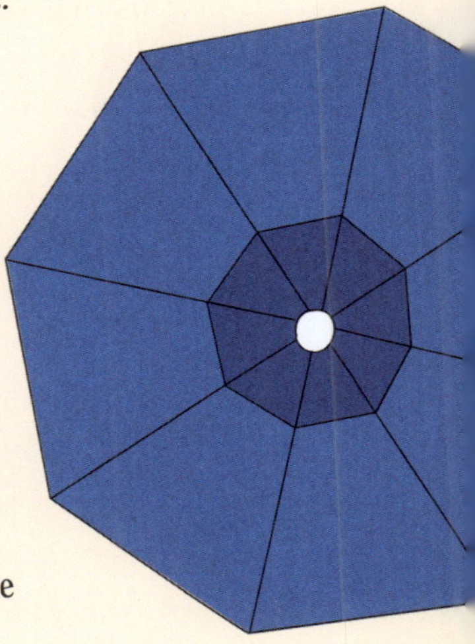

Beach *à la Parisienne*. Even the Chalet du Lac on the small lake in Paris's Bois de Vincennes park changes its look in summer, turning into a sort of vacation resort (but a private one, this time), complete with a beach, foosball tables (*baby-foot*), and bungalows. And all very close to the metro station …

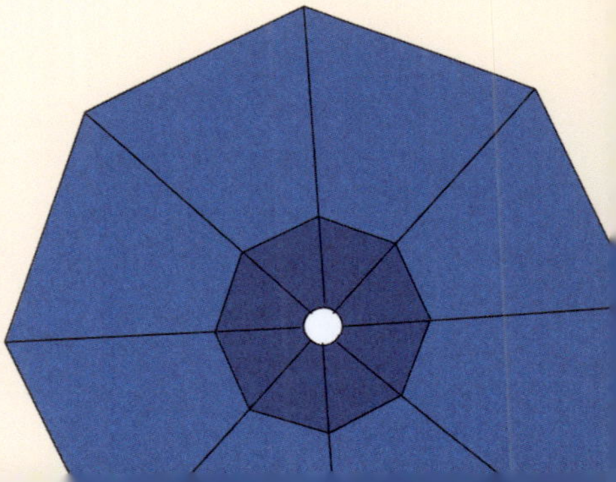

Fête nationale

The French Republic's national holiday is celebrated on July 14 with a host of events. Proceedings begin at **10 A.M. with a** military parade on the Champs-Élysées followed by a review of the troops by the president, before finishing in style with a concert of classical music given beneath the Eiffel Tower and a much-anticipated firework display.

So why July 14? The Loi Raspail (Raspail Law) of 1880 that officially enacted this day as a national holiday does not actually mention the event being commemorated, but it is generally thought to refer to the Storming of the Bastille (1789), the symbol of the end of absolute monarchy.

Fireworks. The show begins at **about 11 P.M. and** lasts for half an hour, with rockets launched from the Jardins du Trocadéro in front of the Eiffel Tower. The best vantage point is the Champ-de-Mars, but given the huge crowds of spectators, you might be better off finding somewhere else with a nice panoramic view, such as the Belvédère de Belleville.

Le Bal des Pompiers (Firemen's Ball). One of the most dangerous events (for male partners!) is held on the evening of July 14, when fire stations open their doors to the public, and especially to women, and turn into rather terrifying nightclubs, with *la drague* (that is, intrusive flirting) an almost mathematical certainty.

Les Grandes Eaux Nocturnes (Night Fountain Show). Visitors to the Palace of Versailles can expect a fabulous show of water, sound, and light from the fountains in the gardens during the evening of July 14, culminating in a firework display over the Grand Canal—just another way of celebrating the national holiday.

Major sporting events

Paris has been a temple of sport for a thousand years. From the *jeu de paume* (a kind of tennis) played since the **eleventh century to the foundation** of the International Olympic Committee in 1894 and today's legendary fixtures that include soccer, tennis, and cycling, Paris has on repeated occasions been at the center of the sporting world.

Paris Saint-Germain. Thanks to massive investment from wealthy Qatari businessman Nasser Al-Khelaifi since 2011, the capital's soccer team has become one of the most successful in Europe, and Paris's Parc des Princes is now a benchmark stadium in the soccer world.

Roland-Garros. The biggest clay court tennis tournament in the world, and one of the most glamorous and popular events in France, was founded in 1925. Matches are held at a complex in the 16th *arrondissement*, so head for the Porte d'Auteuil metro station near the Bois de Boulogne.

The **Tour de France** was first held in 1903 and, along with the Giro d'Italia and the Vuelta di Spagna, has become the most important annual event in cycling, attracting the largest global TV audiences after the Olympic Games and the soccer World Cup. The final stage and the finish on the Champs-Élysées in Paris still exert an iconic fascination.

Paris 2024. Paris was officially unveiled in 2017 as the host city for the Summer Olympics in 2024, the third time in its history that the Games were held here, exactly a hunded years after the last occasion. Some 95 percent of the facilities were already in place and only the Arena Porte de la Chapelle and an Olympic water sports center (in Saint-Denis) had to be built from scratch.

The Paris Marathon. Second only to New York in terms of numbers finishing (Berlin beat Paris in the same year), this classic race has been run every year since 1976. The course has kept to the Right Bank since 2005, taking in such unmissable places as the Champs-Élysées, Place Vendôme, Place de l'Opéra, Rue de Rivoli, Place de la Bastille, and the Pont de Bir-Hakeim.

A-SIDES

1. "Paris, c'est une idée"
(Léo Ferré)

2. "Paris"
(Paolo Conte)

3. "Le Poinçonneur des Lilas"
(Serge Gainsbourg)

4. "La Seine"
(Vanessa Paradis, featuring M)

5. "Le Temps des cathédrales"
(Riccardo Cocciante
and Luc Plamondon)

6. "Parivélib'"
(Philippe Katerine)

7. "Les Bobos"
(Renaud)

8. "Champs-Élysées"
(NOFX), cover

9. "Le Vent"
(Georges Brassens)

10. "Rive Gauche"
(Alain Souchon)

11. "Place des grands hommes"
(Patrick Bruel)

12. "La Bohème"
(Charles Aznavour)

13. "I'm Throwing My Arms Around Paris"
(Morrissey)

14. "Ici Paris"
(Noir Désir)

15. "La Valse d'Amélie"
(Yann Tiersen), orchestral version

16. "The Phantom of the Opera"
(Andrew Lloyd Webber)

17. "La Foule"
(Édith Piaf)

18. "Quatrième de couverture"
(Vincent Delerm)

19. "Parigi con le gambe aperte"
(Gino Paoli and Ricky Gianco)

20. "À Paris sur mer"
(Michel Polnareff)

Paris
je t'aime

Federico Iarlori was born in Ortona in Abruzzo, Italy, in 1983. After taking a degree in modern literature at the Catholic University of Milan, he has lived in France for almost sixteen years, where he is currently bringing up two Italian/French/German children and working as a freelance editor and translator for Art, a public service TV channel. His first novel, *Se una notte a Parigi una tedesca e un italiano* (Giunti) was published in 2020 and he has featured in Ritals, a web series about Italians in France, since 2015.

Monica Lovati is a graphic designer and illustrator who began her career with a focus on visual identity and editorial design projects. She had the privilege of working with Ettore Sottsass, under whose artistic direction she learned a new creative approach that has influenced her thinking and vision. She went on to work as an art director in the worlds of fashion and luxury goods before opening her own studio specializing in visual communications in 2010. She has illustrated Elisabetta Cirillo's *New York Mania* (2019) and Francesca Barra's *A occhio e quanto basta* (2022) for Rizzoli.

Originally published in 2023 by Mondadori Libri S.p.A.

First published in English in 2026
by Rizzoli Universe, a division of
Rizzoli International Publications

Rizzoli International Publications Inc
49 West 27th Street
New York, NY 10001

Rizzoli International Publications UK Ltd
Somerset House, West Wing
Strand, London WC2R 1LA

www.rizzoliusa.com

Publisher: Charles Miers
Associate Publisher: Tina Persaud
Senior Editor: Kristy Richardson
Graphic design and illustrations: Monica Lovati

A CIP catalogue record for this book is available from the British Library.

ISBN 9780789346889

2026 / 1
Printed in Italy

The authorized representative in the EU for safety and compliance is
Mondadori Libri S.p.A., via Gian Battista Vico 42, Milan, Italy, 0123,
www.mondadori.it

Visit us online: Instagram.com/RizzoliBooks
Facebook.com/RizzoliNewYork
Youtube.com/user/RizzoliNY

PEFC Certified
This product is from sustainably managed forests and controlled sources
PEFC
PEFC/18-31-1413
www.pefc.org